EAT WELL
STAY WELL

EAT WELL
STAY WELL

Marguerite Patten

HAMLYN

NOTES

1. Recipes in this book serve 2, unless otherwise stated.

2. Metric and imperial measurements have been calculated
   separately. Use one set of measurements only as they
   are not exact equivalents and are therefore not
   interchangeable.

3. Standard spoon measurements are used in the recipes:
   1 tablespoon = one 15 ml spoon.
   1 teaspoon = one 5 ml spoon.

4. Preheat the oven to the required temperature.

5. Where microwave cooking notes appear under recipes, the
   timings given are based on a microwave cooker with a
   600 watt output.

First published in 1989 by The Hamlyn Publishing Group Limited,
a division of the Octopus Publishing Group,
Michelin House, 81 Fulham Road, London SW3 6RB

ISBN 0 600 56485 1

Produced by Ihasa - printed in Spain

CONTENTS

INTRODUCTION

The years of retirement should be a time to enjoy the increased leisure that now is available and which will allow you to discover new interests and to spend more time on your hobbies. Maybe you have already found out that home decorating or gardening is now a pleasure, rather than a chore and that you have artistic and craft skills you never knew you possessed. Cooking is a craft that can give satisfaction to both the cook and those fortunate enough to sample the results. There is a wide range of foods from around the world in the shops nowadays and it is interesting and stimulating to experiment with these. You will have time to try recipes that seemed 'too much bother' when life was more hectic.

There may be ways in which you will want to change your eating habits to fit into your present lifestyle. It could be a good idea to have a more substantial meal in the middle of the day, rather than at night. This will give you more time to relax.

If you spend holidays abroad, try making in your own kitchen the dishes you have sampled in other countries. Impress your friends with new menus.

You may be cooking most days for just one or two people, after years of preparing family meals. It does mean making adjustments but in this book you will find many dishes that are ideal for smaller households, and even individual portions. You can be slightly selfish and consider your preferences, rather than trying to please all the members of the family.

When the weather is fine why not eat out-of-doors? I have suggested ideas for quickly prepared picnics in this book.

Do not allow the thought of having less money to spend on food depress or worry you. Instead, take a little time to discover the wide range of ingredients that are both inexpensive and delicious. You may well find that you are eating in a more interesting manner and saving money at the same time.

A great deal of advice is given on what we should, or should not, eat as we get older. It is sensible to read, or listen to, information available and appreciate the fact that our diet may need to be changed slightly. This does not mean giving up all the things we have enjoyed in the past or enduring boring and monotonous meals but the right choice of food is an important factor in helping to maintain good health. As an example, it is acknowledged that as we get older our bones tend to become more brittle, hence the fact that an unlucky fall could result in a broken bone, rather than the bruise we probably would have incurred when younger. The food we eat may not stop us tripping over, but it certainly can assist in preventing bones becoming quite as fragile.

Health-giving meals should also be appetising; it is a pleasant thought that the dishes we enjoy play an important part in creating a feeling of well-being. To be really fit enables us to enjoy our lives to the full.

To have a little more time at our disposal to cook meals can be a real boon. It gives one the opportunity to entertain friends and to plan treats for the family when they visit or 'drop in'. This book includes recipes for these special occasions as well as tips to make the preparations as simple and labour-saving as possible.

Various charities find that home-cooked goodies are a successful and popular way of raising money. I have included suitable recipes, for you may feel you would like to use a little of your spare time cooking for a cause that is 'near and dear' to you. Working for a charity is a splendid way of making new friends.

There is so much to enjoy in life as we get older. Good food and good cooking can add to our enjoyment and promote good health. I hope this book will add to your pleasure.

Bon appetit!

Marguerite Patten

INTRODUCTION TO COOKING

Most of you using this book will be experienced cooks and therefore you will be very conversant with the language of cookery. I have, however, included a few basic definitions of culinary terms for those people who have had little time, or need, to cook in the past. These are the facts one should know when preparing or cooking food, for the right method of handling or heating the ingredients can make the difference between a first class result and one that is less good.

The ingredients in the recipes are in both metric and imperial weights and measures. Follow one OR the other, not a combination of both, as they are not interchangeable. In most recipes the quantities are sufficient for two average-size portions. In the part of the book in which dishes for dinner parties or other special occasions are given, starting on page 132, the quantities are for four or more.

As the dishes in this book have been planned to give health-giving as well as enjoyable meals, you will find an indication of special food values at the foot of many recipes.

If you have been used to catering for a larger family you may find it a little difficult at first to adjust your buying habits and cooking to smaller amounts of food. If this means you sometimes have 'leftovers' do not let this worry you; you can turn the extra food into delicious new dishes. In the section on Main Meals you will often find that there is an indication as to where you could cook a double amount of a certain basic food and use this in two entirely different dishes, so saving time and fuel.

Ideas for a sensibly stocked storecupboard and freezer are given on the pages that follow, together with information on equipment and appliances. These can make life easier as we get older and perhaps less agile.

SAFETY FIRST

Many accidents occur in the kitchen; parents take careful safeguards to ensure children are not harmed by falling from a stool, cutting a finger or being burned or scalded. It may be difficult to appreciate the fact that as we get older our agility and our reactions are less efficient, so we need to be just as watchful as when looking after a child. The preparation and cooking of food should be safe, as well as successful.

Check that the height at which you prepare food is right for YOU so you have full control over the actions of chopping, rolling out, etc. It may be better to sit, rather than stand, to carry out these tasks, in which case ensure that the stool or chair is the right height.

If you find that your hands and wrists become tired quickly explore the possibility of electrical appliances, or those for the disabled, to do the hard work for you.

Do not store food and equipment at a height that means you need to stretch or climb on a stool to reach them. Take care when removing dishes from the oven; it is easier if you stand these in a larger roasting tin, for ovenproof ceramics are inclined to be slippery.

Choose the kind of saucepans that have secure handles with no screws that could become loose or hot in cooking. It is a good idea to have those with a handle on either side to balance the weight.

As we get older our sight becomes less keen, so mark containers of food clearly. Do not depend entirely upon the look of the food, a gentle pressure will tell you when a cake is cooked and if you listen carefully you will hear when the liquid is boiling too fast in a stew or under a steamer.

SOME COMMON COOKERY TERMS

○ Boiling – cooking in liquid that bubbles briskly; water boils at 100°C/212°F.
○ Creaming – beating ingredients, often fat and sugar, to blend and aerate. Use a wooden spoon if doing this by hand and stand the bowl on a folded teacloth, so it does not slip.
○ Curdling – term for a mixture that separates. A sauce curdles if overheated when acid wine or lemon juice is mixed with milk.
○ Folding – a gentle 'flicking' movement used when adding sugar to whisked egg whites or flour in a light sponge mixture. Too brisk a movement destroys the light texture.
○ Frying – cooking in hot oil or fat. Drain most fried foods on absorbent kitchen paper before serving.
○ Grilling – a healthy way of cooking. Pre-heat the grill before placing most food underneath. (Bacon rashers are an exception.)
○ Simmering – cooking in liquid at a slightly lower temperature than boiling, i.e. about 82°C/180°F. Most stews should be simmered. If the liquid boils the food could become tough or break up and the liquid evaporate, leaving a burnt pan. Make sure the lid fits tightly on the saucepan if simmering food for a prolonged period.
○ Whisking – a brisk movement used to incorporate air into mixtures or to beat egg whites or cream until stiff. Whisking can make a lumpy sauce smooth. Invest in a strong hand whisk; if you find the vigorous action painful, a small electric portable whisk is the answer. Some of these can also be used on a stand.

YOUR BASIC FOODS

Do not buy an excess of ingredients that you may not use for a very long time. It is tempting to look for bargains, such as large cans of fruit, etc. that seem very cheap. If you are sure you can use all the contents, or freeze the excess, then it will be a bargain, but if you do not use it all money has been wasted.

In The Storecupboard
○ Beverages – you need tea, coffee and cocoa or chocolate powder. If you prefer ground coffee, do not buy too large an amount unless vacuum packed.
○ Canned foods – one or two cans of soup, fish such as sardines, tuna or salmon (which can make a good hot or cold meal), fruit (you can buy this canned in natural juice), vegetables, such as butter and haricot beans.
○ Cereals – the crispness can be lost if the packet is not kept closed; bran is considered an important cereal for providing edible fibre.
○ Cornflour – useful for thickening liquids instead of flour; a good ingredient in some sauces (see page 26) and certain biscuits.
○ Dried fruit – of various kinds.
○ Flavourings – such as essences, soy sauce, yeast extract.
○ Flour – wholemeal, brown and white flours are used in recipes in this book. If you prefer plain flour, you will need baking powder for some recipes. Do not buy too large a quantity if you bake rarely.
○ Herbs – although fresh herbs are far better you may need dried herbs in winter or when fresh are unavailable.
○ Oatmeal – in some form; its value is described on page 131. Modern rolled oats enable you to make porridge quickly and easily (see page 19).
○ Pasta – macaroni, spaghetti and other pasta shapes are an excellent basis for satis-fying meals. Try wholemeal pasta for extra flavour and food value.
○ Rice – another first class food that can be varied in many ways. Brown rice has more flavour and fibre than white. Choose long-grain rice for savoury dishes, short-grain rice for puddings.
○ Seasonings – salt, pepper, mustard.
○ Spices – a selection of various spices, see recipes.
○ Sugar – although sugar is used sparingly in many recipes in this book, you will need several kinds, see recipes.
○ Vinegar – white wine vinegar is better for salad dressings but malt vinegar can be used.

In The Freezer
○ Bread – if you slice the bread before freezing then wrapping, it is easy to peel off the number of slices required. When you make breadcrumbs pack and freeze the surplus.
○ Cakes – if an economical recipe, freeze the cake to save it becoming stale; slice before freezing, as suggested under Bread.
○ Cheese – it is a good idea to freeze any leftover or extra cheese so it does not deteriorate.
○ Fish – one or two packets of commercially frozen fish – never freeze fish yourself unless you are 100% certain it is fresh.
○ Fruit and fruit purées – for desserts or sauces.
○ Meat – packed in small portions.
○ Poultry – chicken portions, turkey breast portions.
○ Vegetables – if you buy large packets make sure the vegetables are free-flowing so you can take out just enough for your needs.
Never freeze food that is not very fresh. Put ready-frozen food into your freezer as soon as you can after buying it. Commercially cooked and chilled food must be eaten as quickly as possible after purchase.

Pizzas are an ideal way to use storecupboard ingredients (see pages 102–103 for recipes)

CHOOSING KITCHEN EQUIPMENT

Major Appliances

These are the expensive pieces of equipment that should give years of satisfactory service, so select them with care.

Cooker

If you are moving to smaller premises and choosing new equipment consider certain factors about your new cooker.

Do you need a full-sized model? A small compact cooker may suit your purpose, especially if you have a microwave cooker.

If you find it difficult to bend down to take dishes from the oven it might be worth while considering a built-in oven at a convenient height together with separate electric hotplates or a gas hob.

Refrigerator

A refrigerator is an essential appliance for the safe storage of perishable foods. If buying a new model consider a combined refrigerator and freezer, which takes up less floor space than two separate appliances.

While you can obtain refrigerators to fit under a working surface, this could be inconvenient if you find bending down not as easy as you would wish. In this case try to avoid such a model unless you are very short of space in the kitchen.

A refrigerator can be built into kitchen units, just like an oven and is at an ideal height for the easy removal of food and for cleaning the refrigerator.

Freezer

A freezer, or combined freezer and refrigerator, is just as beneficial to a household of one or two people as a more generous-sized model is to a larger family. You will find suggestions for some of the basic foods that can be stored in the freezer on page 10. In addition, if you are making a dish that is a great favourite, you can cook two or three times the quantity given in the recipe, enjoy some of the freshly cooked food and freeze the remainder in suitable-sized containers. This means you will have food available for the days when you do not feel like shopping or cooking. Home-cooked food is not only better than commercial convenience food, but, in most cases it is a great deal cheaper.

Microwave Cooker

This modern approach to cooking is ideal for a smaller household, for it is at its most efficient when dealing with individual or smaller portions of food. There may be many occasions when you can prepare the meal in the microwave cooker without using the larger cooker, so saving fuel, since a microwave cooker uses relatively little electricity.

When purchasing a microwave consider the possibility of investing in a model that combines both conventional and microwave cooking facilities. Obviously this will be more expensive than standard microwaves. Some people, with limited kitchen space who cook for a small household, find they can manage to prepare meals with one of the combination microwave cookers plus hotplates.

The brief hints under the recipes apply to a standard microwave cooker (not the combination model). Any timings given are based on a cooker with a 600 watt output.

A point to consider when using a microwave cooker is that you can cut down on the amount of fat and salt used. If you are adapting a recipe, reduce the amount of fat by 50% and the salt to a minimum.

Electric Mixer

An electric mixer is a great asset for creaming and whisking mixtures; it can be used to rub fat into flour or knead a yeast mixture. If you are finding these tasks difficult to perform due to rheumatism or arthritis in your hands, it is sensible to consider investing in such a mixer. Sizes and prices vary considerably.

Liquidizer

This is a splendid appliance for producing smooth soups or making vegetable or fruit purées. It can be used to make small amounts of breadcrumbs, pâté, etc.

Food Processor

A food processor is a wonderful appliance for chopping, grating and slicing a wide variety of ingredients and for making purées of vegetables, fruit, etc. It can take the place of a liquidizer in preparing soups, although the result is not as smooth a mixture. The food processor can be used to knead mixtures. It can be used for cake making, although you do not have such a good result as when using an electric mixer. It is better to choose the All-in-One Method of cake making, described on page 121 and 125 rather than the more traditional one.

Equipment and Appliances

Handle gadgets in shops before you buy, to make certain they will do a satisfactory job FOR YOU. The following are not gadgets but basic small appliances and equipment.

○ Board – for chopping; most laminated surfaces are spoiled by this action, so choose a wooden board.

○ Can opener – some hand-operated models are very difficult to use if you have arthritis, so choose carefully. Electrically operated models are not very expensive.

○ Casseroles – consider buying the kind of flame-proof casseroles than can be used as pans on top of the cooker as well as in the oven. These are rather heavy, so always choose one with two handles, so you can use both hands when lifting it.

○ Fish slice – for removing food from a pan; use a silicone fish slice for a silicone pan.

○ Frying pan – it is stressed by nutritionalists that people of all ages should cut down on fat, so use a frying pan as infrequently as possible. Silicone treated (non-stick) pans mean you can reduce the amount of fat used by at least 50%.

○ Grater – if chopping food finely (such as onions) is becoming difficult, try grating them instead. A stainless steel grater is easier to keep clean and is stronger than those made of other metals or plastic.

○ Knives – make sure you choose well-balanced knives that are easy to hold – you need a small sharp knife for preparing vegetables, although a vegetable peeler is safer and easier to use. You also need a larger sharp knife for carving and slicing.

○ Saucepans – see the comments under Casseroles and under Safety First, page 9.

○ Steamer – an excellent utensil for saving fuel, as you can cook several different dishes on one gas ring or electric hotplate. Check that the steamer fits securely over the saucepan in which water will be heated.

○ Stool – or combined stool and steps, or a kitchen chair. Check that this is easy to move but is the ideal height for sitting and working. It is essential that it is well-balanced and not likely to tip over.

○ Universal opener – many jars have tightly fitting lids which need considerable manual strength to remove. This attachment does it with great ease.

START THE DAY RIGHT

There are very decided views about the best way to start the day. Some people stress that they habitually enjoy a really sustaining and traditional breakfast; this leads one to assume they mean a cooked meal.

Other people, both young and old, shudder at the thought of food first thing in the morning and say they have a hasty cup of tea or coffee and that is all they require. Quite frequently, though, the non-breakfast eaters add 'Of course, I enjoy breakfast on holiday'.

A third group, who are fairly usual nowadays, have a light meal of cereal and toast.

What is a perfect start to the day? Nutritionalists stress that a nourishing meal first thing in the morning is important. If you miss breakfast you are likely to feel lacking in energy by mid-morning. That does not mean it has to be a cooked breakfast, in fact a meal that has an over-generous amount of fat should be avoided. If you choose fruit or fruit juice, followed by a well-chosen cereal and toast, preferably made from wholemeal bread, you can claim quite correctly that you have started the day well.

When one has more time breakfast can be a pleasant and leisurely meal. You can choose the hour at which you eat it – no rushing to work or making sure every member of the family leaves home with all their needs satisfied.

You may feel like enjoying the meal better if you carry out a few household tasks first. If you are an ardent gardener there is nothing more pleasant than spending a little time in the garden before you come in to the first meal of the day.

The choice of food you could serve is very varied; there are no hard and fast rules, simply try to have health-giving, interesting and varied menus.

Muesli with fresh fruit: an excellent start to the day (recipes page 16)

14

TAKE YOUR CHOICE

Here are some of the foods to consider when deciding what to eat for breakfast.

○ Bread – people who are anxious to lose weight are inclined to think that this important and nutritious food should be restricted because of its calorific value. 25 g/1 oz of white, wholemeal or brown bread has only about 70 Kcal/293 Kjoules. A slice of bread from a medium loaf is just over this. The 'danger' is the amount of butter or margarine and preserves used on the bread or toast. If you are anxious to restrict fat and calories, use a low fat spread.
○ Wholemeal or brown bread is higher in fibre than white. Easy recipes for making bread are given on page 116 and Baking Powder Cobs in this chapter.
○ Cereals – there is a wide range available: look for those high in fibre and low in sugar. You can choose skimmed or semi-skimmed milk to serve over the cereals to reduce the fat. Recipes for porridge and Muesli are on page 19 and this page.
○ Eggs – cooked in various ways (see pages 87 and 88).
○ Fish – there are many fish dishes that make an excellent breakfast dish – white fish, cod's roe, herring roes, etc. To reduce your salt intake rinse smoked (salted) fish like haddock and kippers in plenty of cold water before cooking.
○ Fruit and fruit juices – whole fruit has more fibre; unsweetened fruit juices can be obtained. Oranges provide important vitamin C, as explained on page 131.
○ Meat – bacon and sausages are favourite breakfast foods. Choose green (unsmoked) bacon which has less salt; you can obtain low fat sausages, if you prefer.
○ Yogurt – of various kinds; spend a little time reading labels when you buy these to ascertain whether the product has a high fat or high sugar content. On pages 82–3 you will find directions for making yogurt.

MUESLI

There are many commercial versions of this uncooked breakfast dish, which originated in a famous Swiss health clinic. The advantage of making your own muesli is that you can add what pleases YOU to the rolled oats, which are the basic ingredient. The amounts given make 2 average portions.

Blend 3 tablespoons uncooked rolled oats with 2 tablespoons seedless raisins or sultanas or sliced uncooked dried apricots or figs; add 1 or 2 tablespoons whole or chopped or ground nuts, a diced or grated dessert apple or segments of other fresh fruit or cooked or canned fruit. Blend with enough milk or natural or flavoured yogurt or fresh fruit juice or liquid from the cooked or canned fruit to moisten.

VARIATIONS:
Add a sprinkling of bran.
Add sugar or honey to taste.
For a more moist texture, soften the oats with the milk or yogurt or fruit juice; stand in the refrigerator overnight.
For a nuttier taste, toast the oats as suggested in the recipe on page 82.

NUTRITIONAL VALUE: An excellent source of fibre plus vitamin C if fresh fruit is used. The dried fruit gives natural sugar.

Poached kippers (top) and Lemon cod's roe (recipes page 18)

FRUIT SUPREME

1 grapefruit
1 orange
1 dessert apple
1 banana

Cut the peel and pith from the grapefruit and orange; do this over a basin so no juice is wasted. Divide the citrus fruit into segments, discarding the skin and pips. Slice the apple, discarding the peel if wished. Peel and slice the banana. Mix the fruit and put into glasses with any juice from the citrus fruits.

VARIATIONS:
Use the citrus fruits with seasonal fresh fruit or cooked fruit.

NUTRITIONAL VALUE: An excellent and refreshing way to start the day; the citrus fruit provides vitamin C.

POACHED KIPPERS

2 large or 4 small kippers
little freshly ground pepper

Put the fish into a large dish. Pour boiling water over the fish, add a little pepper. Cover tightly, allow to stand for about 5 minutes. The fish will be lightly, but perfectly, cooked. Drain and serve. If you like crisp kippers you could then brush them with a few drops of oil and place under a preheated grill for 2 or 3 minutes.

NOTE: This method of cooking keeps the smell of fish out of the kitchen. You could cook extra fish for the pâté and sandwich filling given on pages 24 and 86 at the same time.

FREEZING: Cook frozen kippers in this way.
MICROWAVE: Put the kippers on a flat dish, cover and cook on **Full Power**. 2 large kippers take approx. 3–4 minutes.
NUTRITIONAL VALUE: The method of cooking extracts surplus salt. The fish is less oily. Good source of protein.

LEMON COD'S ROE

225 g/8 oz uncooked fresh cod's roe
salt and pepper
½ lemon
25 g/1 oz butter or margarine
2 tablespoons soft breadcrumbs

Wash the cod's roe in cold water, put into a saucepan with cold water to cover, salt, pepper and a squeeze of lemon juice. Bring the water to the boil, lower the heat and simmer for 10 minutes, strain then skin and slice the roe. Put into a flameproof dish, add a little more lemon juice. Melt the butter or margarine, mix with the crumbs. Place over the cod's roe and heat under the grill for a few minutes.

VARIATIONS:
Buy cooked cod's roe, slice, add the lemon juice and proceed as above.
White fish can be served in the same way.
Bacon and Cod's Roe: Slice the cooked cod's roe, place in the grill pan, top with lean bacon rashers; grill until the bacon is crisp.

FREEZING: The uncooked roe freezes well, cooked roe is inclined to lose flavour.
MICROWAVE: Cover the uncooked roe with water, add the seasoning and lemon juice, cook for about 6 minutes on **Full Power**. The roe is cooked when opaque.
NUTRITIONAL VALUE: This fish is high in protein and low in fat.

EASY PORRIDGE

Porridge makes a warming and nutritious start to the day. Modern rolled oats mean the dish is prepared easily and quickly. To save the bother of weighing the oats use a cup or measure. The following quantities, which give medium portions for 2 people, are based upon an average breakfast cup, or a 300 ml/½ pint measure. The average teacup is about 150 ml/¼ pint.

Pour 2 cups water, or milk, or a mixture of milk and water, into a strong pan. If you prefer a less stiff porridge increase the amount of liquid to 2½ cups or measures.

Sprinkle 1 level cup of oats on to the cold liquid; add a small pinch of salt. Bring the liquid to the boil, stirring all the time, then lower the heat and simmer for 3 minutes, or as directed on the packet of oats. Stir from time to time.

The porridge is then ready to serve. You can add sugar or honey and milk or natural or flavoured yogurt, or see below.

VARIATIONS:
If using the thicker form of wholemeal oats you will need to increase both the amount of liquid and allow a little longer cooking time, so follow the packet details.
Flavour the mixture as it cooks, e.g. add a little dried fruit or diced apple or a pinch of ground cinnamon or other spice.
Top cooked porridge with sliced fresh or cooked fruit or a sprinkling of bran.

To avoid continual stirring, as in the method above, use the same quantities of liquid and oats. Bring the liquid to the boil, sprinkle on the oats. Stir briskly for 1 minute. Remove the pan from the heat, cover it tightly, leave standing for 2 or 3 minutes then stir and serve the porridge. This method is not suitable for thicker oats.

MICROWAVE: Use the same quantities as those given in the recipe above. Blend the cold liquid and oats in a large bowl. Do not cover. Place in the microwave cooker and cook for 3½ to 4 minutes on **Full Power**. Stir briskly, allow to stand for 1 minute then serve. This porridge may appear a little thin when it comes from the microwave but it thickens with standing.
NUTRITIONAL VALUE: Rolled oats, like all forms of oatmeal, are an excellent source of soluble fibre (see page 131).

BAKING POWDER COBS

100 g/4 oz self-raising white flour, or plain flour sifted with 1 teaspoon baking powder
pinch salt
15 g/½ oz margarine or low fat spread
approximately 4 tablespoons milk

Preheat the oven to very hot (230°C, 450°F, Gas Mark 8). Blend the flour and salt, rub in the margarine, or the spread. Gradually blend in the milk to give a soft rolling consistency. Form into 6 balls with floured fingers, then place on the baking tray. Bake for approximately 10 minutes, until well risen, crisp and golden.
Makes 6

VARIATIONS:
Wholemeal Cobs: Use wholemeal instead of white flour with slightly more milk.
Oaty Cobs: Use 75 g/3 oz flour and 25 g/1 oz rolled oats. If using self-raising flour add ½ teaspoon baking powder. Use 1 teaspoon baking powder with plain flour. You will need slightly more milk to give the desired consistency. Roll into balls, brush with milk, coat in rolled oats. Bake for about 12 minutes.

PLANNING MAIN MEALS

The main meal of the day is important, for it should provide many of the important nutrients needed each day. This meal tends to entail more detailed shopping and cooking than do other occasions. All too often people living alone are inclined to say 'it is too much trouble to cook for one person'. Do not adopt this attitude, for it is very important that you have good nourishing food and enjoy your meals.

There are many ways in which the preparation of the meal can be simplified. In several recipes the food is cooked in a foil parcel – a method adapted from the French way 'en papillote'. The good flavour of the ingredients is confined within the foil and there is the minimum of washing-up afterwards. What could be easier?

The section on vegetable dishes suggests ways of utilising few pots and pans. Another point covered is the way in which you can buy and prepare a basic food and turn it into two entirely diffcrent dishes.

It is extra work, but a pleasant challenge, to prepare food that will be enjoyed by other people. Every cook appreciates hearing the words 'thank you, that was a lovely meal'. Why not form an unofficial luncheon club where several friends take it in turns to prepare the meal? If this sounds a little bit like hard work, then adopt the American idea. You meet at various homes in turn; each person brings part of the meal, so everyone shares the work, and you eat in pleasant company.

The recipes in this chapter cover all the courses from starters and soups to main dishes of various kinds and easy, but delicious, puddings and desserts. Some recipes give hints on preparing the dishes ahead. Information on freezing and microwave cooking follows each recipe where relevant.

Avocado pâté (top) and Avocado and grapefruit cocktail (recipes page 23)

STARTERS AND SOUPS

An interesting starter or soup can transform a rather ordinary meal into an exciting one. If well-chosen it also adds nutritional value to the meal. The starter or soup should be light if it is to be followed with both a main dish and a dessert.

Fruit in various forms, as suggested on this and the following pages, small portions of salad, vegetable and fish dishes all make excellent starts to the meal. Most people enjoy a pâté and there are several recipes, based upon fruit, vegetables, fish and meat in this chapter, and on page 147.

If you are not particularly fond of desserts why not have a starter or soup and main dish? If, on the other hand, you have a small appetite and love the sweet course, then plan a nourishing starter or soup and follow this with a pudding.

The soup dishes in this book range from light and low calorie recipes to those that are sufficiently satisfying to make a complete meal. Quite often you can use those tiresome leftovers as the basis for an appetising soup.

Do not overcook vegetable soups, for you should try and retain all the fresh flavour of the various ingredients. The same rule applies if the soup contains fish, for this loses texture, as well as flavour, if cooked for too long a period.

Microwave cooking of soups

The high proportion of liquid used in soups means that the saving of time when cooking in the microwave is not as great as when cooking more solid foods.

Always chop onions and other firm textured ingredients into very small and even-sized pieces; use slightly less liquid unless stated to the contrary.

Ways to serve fruit

The fruit one serves at the beginning of a meal should have a rather sharp flavour so that it is refreshing and will not spoil your appetite for the rest of the meal. This is why the dressings suggested in several recipes, where fruit is an important ingredient, have more lemon juice in proporton to the oil than usual. This also reduces the fat content of the dish, an important consideration if you are calorie-conscious.

Fruit juices can be mixed together to give a new taste. Try a combination of orange and tomato juices or apple and orange or pineapple and grapefruit. More piquant flavoured Fruit Sorbets, which you will find on page 143, provide an original start to the meal and have the advantage that they can be prepared well ahead.

The Fruit Soup on page 32 can be made throughout the year, and you can vary the flavour according to the fruits that are in season. This is a wonderful meal starter if your appetite is a little jaded. Fruit also forms an important part in many salads, improving the flavour and look of the dish. It also prevents the need to buy the more usual salad ingredients at the time of the year when they are expensive.

A new look to old favourites

Serve grapefruit hot. Halve the fruit, spread the cut surfaces with honey and ground cinnamon or moisten with sherry and top with chopped nuts and brown sugar. Grill for 1 or 2 minutes.

Top melon slices with a little ground ginger and honey and heat for 1 or 2 minutes under the grill.

Melon blends well with salami or similar meats or with prawns or other shellfish.

AVOCADO PÂTÉ

1 ripe avocado
1 tablespoon lemon juice
2 tablespoons fromage frais (see page 130)
  or natural yogurt
few drops Tabasco sauce (optional)
salt and pepper

Halve the avocado, scoop out the pulp and mash this with the lemon juice then add the fromage frais or yogurt. Add the Tabasco sauce to give a hot flavour and a little seasoning. Spoon into individual dishes and serve with crispbread or hot toast.

VARIATION:
Blend the avocado pulp with a skinned and deseeded fresh tomato instead of the fromage frais or yogurt.

NUTRITIONAL VALUE: The avocado adds protein to a meal.

AVOCADO AND GRAPEFRUIT COCKTAILS

For the lemon dressing:
1 tablespoon soya or sunflower seed or corn
  oil
1 tablespoon lemon juice
salt and pepper
1 teaspoon sugar

1 small grapefruit, preferably pink variety
1 small ripe avocado
few lettuce leaves

Mix the ingredients for the dressing together. Cut away the peel and pith from the grapefruit. Do this over the basin of dressing so that the excess juice blends with the dressing. Cut away the grapefruit segments. Halve the avocado, remove the stone and pull away the peel. Dice the pulp; add to the dressing. Finely shred the lettuce and put into glasses or dishes. Top with the grapefruit segments then the avocado and dressing.
Serves 2–3

VARIATIONS:
Use orange segments or diced melon instead of grapefruit or use grapefruit canned in natural juice.
Avocado and Mushroom Cocktails: Use sliced very fresh button mushrooms instead of grapefruit.
Avocado and Prawn Cocktails: Use peeled prawns instead of grapefruit.

ORANGE AND GRAPE BASKETS

1 large orange
100 g/4 oz grapes, preferably seedless
2 tablespoons dry sherry or white wine
few mint leaves

Cut the orange through the centre, scoop out the segments of fruit, discard the pips, save the orange halves. Cut away the skin with kitchen scissors. Mix the orange segments with whole or halved grapes and the sherry or white wine. Add the mint. Chill well and spoon back into the orange halves.

VARIATIONS:
Use diced avocado, grapefruit segments or seasonal fruit with the orange.
Melon Baskets: Use a small ripe melon instead of the orange.

NUTRITIONAL VALUE: An ideal way to enjoy fresh fruit with fibre and vitamin C.

EASY PÂTÉS

The following recipes make interesting pâtés with a delicate light texture. These pâtés deteriorate quickly, as they have no butter coating and they do not freeze well.

KIPPER PÂTÉ

3 large kippers, cooked as on page 18
1 tablespoon horseradish cream
1 garlic clove, crushed
½–1 tablespoon lemon juice
4 tablespoons natural yogurt
black pepper

Remove all the flesh from the kippers, discard the bones and skin. Flake the flesh then blend with the other ingredients in a food processor if wished.
Serves 4

VARIATIONS:
Smoked Mackerel Pâté: Use 2 smoked mackerel fillets instead of kippers. These do not require cooking.
White Fish and Watercress Pâté: Use 175 g/6 oz cooked white fish instead of the kippers and 1 tablespoon mayonnaise instead of horseradish cream. Add 25 g/1 oz melted butter or margarine and 3 tablespoons finely chopped watercress leaves.

GIBLET PÂTÉ

cooked giblets from a medium sized chicken
2 or 3 cocktail onions
few sprigs parsley
15 g/½ oz butter or margarine, melted
1 tablespoon sherry
4 tablespoons natural yogurt
salt and pepper

Remove the flesh from the neck of the bird, cut the heart and liver into small pieces. Put all the ingredients into a food processor and blend well. Leave for 1 or 2 hours in the refrigerator. Serve with hot toast.

CARROT PÂTÉ

225 g/8 oz young carrots, cut into thin slices
* (weight when prepared)*
1 medium onion, finely chopped or grated
1 garlic clove, crushed
salt and pepper
25 g/1 oz butter or margarine, melted
100 g/4 oz cottage cheese, sieved
2 tablespoons finely chopped parsley
1 teaspoon sesame seeds (optional)

Bring a little water to the boil, add the carrots, onion and garlic with a little seasoning. Cover the pan and cook briskly until the carrots are just tender. Do not overcook these. Strain the vegetables, put into a food processor with the butter or margarine and cheese. Switch on until smooth, then blend in the parsley. Serve topped with the sesame seeds.
Serves 4

VARIATIONS:
Other vegetable pâtés: Use cooked haricot or other beans, celeriac, lentils or a mixture of vegetables.
To save using a food processor grate the vegetables, where possible, before cooking. They are then very easy to mash smoothly.

NUTRITIONAL VALUE: If using-up cooked vegetables much of the value is lost but you still have a relatively low calorie but satisfying dish.

Making the Carrot pâté (top) and Kipper pâté (recipes this page)

CREAMY SOUPS

These soups are an ideal way of using up small portions of cooked fish, poultry or vegetables you may have in the refrigerator. The basis for the soup is a thin White sauce (see page 75), but with more liquid, plus 100–150 g/4–5 oz cooked food and flavourings as given in the recipes.

You can choose low fat spread, rather than butter or margarine to make the sauce. In this case follow the 'all-in-one' method given on page 75. Instead of all milk you could use some fish or chicken or vegetable stock, if this is available. This emphasises the flavour of the basic ingredient. The use of cornflour, rather than flour, in the sauce means it thickens more quickly and fewer calories are added.

Obviously you can cook a small amount of vegetables first, strain these, use the stock in the soup, then add the prepared vegetables. An exception to this rule is when making a spinach soup with raw spinach (see right).

SPINACH SOUP

For the sauce:
25 g/1 oz butter or margarine or low fat
    spread
25 g/1 oz plain flour or 15 g/½ oz cornflour
600 ml/1 pint milk or 450 ml/¾ pint milk and
    150 ml/¼ pint spinach stock

100–150 g/4–5 oz cooked spinach
½ tablespoon lemon juice
pinch ground or grated nutmeg
salt and pepper

Make the sauce, following the directions on page 75. Use plain flour in all sauces if possible and follow the all-in-one method for low fat spread.

Chop the spinach finely, add to the sauce. Heat as quickly as possible, stirring well during this time; add the lemon juice, nutmeg and seasoning.

VARIATIONS:
Use uncooked spinach. There is no need to increase the amount of liquid in the sauce to compensate for the extra cooking time. Shred the spinach leaves, put into the sauce; cook steadily until tender then sieve or liquidize the soup and reheat.
Frozen chopped spinach is ideal for this soup. Do not defrost the spinach. Put a small block into the hot sauce, cook steadily, scraping the spinach away from the block as it cooks.
Use 5 tablespoons less milk in the sauce. Add 5 tablespoons natural yogurt or single cream just before serving, heat gently and do not allow to boil.
Top the cooked soup with natural yogurt or cottage or curd cheese and flaked almonds.
Give more flavour to the sauce for this, and the other vegetable soups, by cooking a finely chopped or grated onion in the fat before making the sauce. Low fat spread is not suitable for this purpose. Increase the butter or margarine to 40 g/1½ oz.
Cauliflower Soup: Follow the method for making the Spinach soup but use cooked cauliflower. Save a few tiny florets for garnish. This soup is nicer if sieved or liquidized and reheated. A topping of cottage, curd or grated cheese turns it into a complete meal.

MICROWAVE: The sauce can be made in the microwave on **Full Power** (see the hints on page 75), the vegetables added and the soup reheated. The amount of liquid needed in the sauce is the same as in the recipe left.

ASPARAGUS SOUP

Sauce as under Spinach soup (see left),
using 450 ml/¾ pint milk and 150 ml/
¼ pint chicken or asparagus stock
chicken or asparagus stock
100–150 g/4–5 oz cooked or canned
asparagus spears
½ tablespoon lemon juice
pinch cayenne pepper
salt and pepper
little cream or natural yogurt

Prepare the sauce. Cut the tender tips from the asparagus, put on one side for garnish. Chop the spears, blend with the sauce then sieve or liquidize until a smooth purée. Heat until nearly boiling, add the lemon juice and seasoning. Top with the cream or yogurt and the asparagus tips.

VARIATIONS:
Artichoke Soup: Cooked Jerusalem artichokes make a delicious soup. Proceed as for the Asparagus Soup above. As this is a very white-looking soup, top with plenty of chopped parsley or chives. Artichokes have a strong taste, so make the sauce with all milk or milk and chicken stock, rather than liquid from cooking the vegetable.
Chicken Soup: Make the sauce (see Spinach Soup, left), but try to use 300 ml/½ pint milk and 300 ml/½ pint chicken stock. Cut the cooked chicken into small shreds, add to the sauce and heat. You can make the soup more interesting by adding blanched flaked almonds and cooked sweetcorn or a selection of diced cooked vegetables or tiny pieces of cooked stuffing. Top the soup with chopped parsley, chives or rosemary and blanched flaked almonds or snippets of crisp bacon.
Creamy Vegetable Soup: Make the sauce (see Spinach soup, left). Add a selection of neatly diced cooked vegetables. You could use about 150 g/5 oz puréed cooked peas, carrots or other vegetables instead. As this will thicken the sauce, use only 1 level tablespoon flour or ½ level tablespoon cornflour when making the sauce.
Smoked Haddock Soup: This is an ideal way of using up about 150 g/5 oz cooked smoked haddock and makes a simple variation of the famous Scottish soup 'Cullen Skink'. Heat 40 g/1½ oz butter or margarine in a pan, add a finely chopped or grated small onion, cook gently for 5 minutes, stir in the 25 g/1 oz flour or 15 g/½ oz cornflour then add 450 ml/¾ pint haddock stock (or use all milk). When the sauce has thickened add a diced cooked potato and the flaked haddock. Heat together.

LEEK AND POTATO CREAM

25 g/1 oz butter or margarine
1 good-sized potato, peeled and chopped
3 medium leeks, peeled and chopped
300 ml/½ pint milk
300 ml/½ pint chicken stock
salt and pepper
4 tablespoons single cream or natural
yogurt
chopped chives

Melt the butter or margarine and toss the vegetables in this. Add the milk and chicken stock and seasoning. Cover the pan and cook for 15 minutes. Sieve or liquidize the ingredients. Reheat, without boiling, adding 4 tablespoons single cream or natural yogurt. Top with chopped chives.

VARIATION:
Vichyssoise: Chill the sieved or liquidized ingredients then blend with the cream or natural yogurt and a little white wine. Top with chopped chives.

SOUPS MAKE A MEAL

The following soups are very satisfying. They can be served as a light main dish if followed by a dessert or fruit.

SCALLOP CHOWDER

1 large or 2 small scallops
1 lean bacon rasher, de-rinded and chopped
300 ml/½ pint water
1 small onion, finely chopped or grated
1 small potato, cut into 6 mm/¼ inch dice
1 teaspoon lemon juice
salt and pepper
1 level teaspoon cornflour
150 ml/¼ pint milk
pinch celery salt
To garnish:
2 lemon rings
little paprika

Wash the scallop(s) in cold water and cut into 1.5 cm/½ inch pieces. Put the bacon, plus the bacon rind, into a saucepan, heat for 2 minutes then remove the bacon rind. Add the water, bring to the boil then put in the onion, potato, lemon juice and a little salt and pepper. Simmer for 8 to 10 minutes, or until the vegetables are nearly soft. Add the scallop(s) and simmer for 2 to 3 minutes. The vegetables should be tender, but unbroken. Blend the cornflour with the milk; stir into the ingredients in the saucepan and continue stirring over a low heat until the soup has thickened. Add the celery salt. Spoon into soup cups and top with the lemon rings and paprika.

VARIATION:
Fish Chowder: Use 150 g/5 oz skinned and diced white fish instead of the scallop(s). Allow 4 to 5 minutes cooking time.

MICROWAVE: Allow approximately the same cooking time on FULL POWER and same liquid content.
NUTRITIONAL VALUE: This soup makes a satisfying meal with an adequate amount of protein. The calorific value can be lowered if skimmed milk is used. The use of cornflour, rather than flour, also lowers the calories (see page 75).

LENTIL AND LEEK CHOWDER

750 ml/1¼ pints bacon stock (see page 152), or water
75 g/3 oz lentils
3 small leeks, thinly sliced
2 tender celery stalks, thinly sliced
salt and pepper
2 small carrots, finely sliced or grated

Pour the stock or water into a saucepan, add the lentils; allow to stand for 1 hour. This stage is not essential, but it does shorten the cooking time by 10 to 15 minutes. Add half the leeks, half the celery, a very little salt and good shake of pepper. Cover the pan and simmer for 40 minutes or until the lentils are tender. Sieve or liquidize the soup, then return the smooth mixture to the saucepan. Add the rest of the leeks and celery. Cook for 10 minutes.

FREEZING: The soup has a better texture if the rest of the leeks and celery are added after defrosting.
MICROWAVE: Allow only 600 ml/1 pint liquid. Cook for 25 to 30 minutes on **Full Power** then add the remaining leeks and celery and cook for 6 minutes.
NUTRITIONAL VALUE: A dish that is high in protein.

Scallop chowder (top – recipe this page) and Leek consommé (recipe page 31)

LENTIL SOUP MILANAISE

750 ml/1¼ pints lamb or bacon stock (see
    pages 55 and 152), or water
75 g/3 oz lentils
2 medium onions, finely chopped or grated
1 small parsley sprig
salt and pepper
2 medium tomatoes, skinned and diced
½ teaspoon finely chopped oregano or
    marjoram

Pour the stock or water into a saucepan, add the lentils; allow to stand for 1 hour. This stage is not essential but it does shorten the cooking time by 10 to 15 minutes. Cover the pan and simmer for 20 minutes; add the onions, the parsley and a very little salt and pepper. Continue cooking for 10 minutes then put in the tomatoes and the remaining herbs. Cook for a further 10 minutes; remove the parsley.

VARIATIONS:
To enhance the tomato flavour, add 1 or 2 teaspoons of tomato purée.
For a more pronounced flavour, add 1 or 2 crushed garlic cloves.
Sieve or liquidize the soup after cooking to give a puréed soup.
Top the soup with natural yogurt.
Curried Lentil Soup: Add 2 teaspoons curry powder or paste to the stock, and a peeled and diced dessert apple.

FREEZING: The smooth puréed soup freezes best; whisk well when defrosted.
MICROWAVE: Allow only 600 ml/1 pint liquid. Cook the lentils for 15 minutes on **Full Power**; then another 7 minutes after adding the onions, etc. Finally add the tomatoes and cook for a further 7 minutes.
NUTRITIONAL VALUE: Another soup that is high in protein.

PIQUANT CAULIFLOWER SOUP

¼ small raw cauliflower
300 ml/½ pint water
1 small onion, finely chopped or grated
1 small potato, finely chopped or grated
pinch ground mace
salt and pepper
pinch cayenne pepper
pinch celery salt
150 ml/¼ pint milk
1 tablespoon finely chopped chives

Break the cauliflower head into very small florets. Bring the water to the boil, add any tough stalks from the cauliflower to the water, cover the pan and cook for 10 minutes. This gives you a very pleasant stock. Lift the stalks from the liquid then add the onion and potato with the mace and the seasonings. Cook for 5 minutes, add the cauliflower florets and milk; continue cooking for 5 to 6 minutes. Add the chives.

VARIATIONS:
Top the soup with a little grated cheese.
For a purée soup follow the recipe above, remove a few cooked florets for garnish. Sieve or liquidize the other ingredients, reheat and top with cauliflower and chives.
Use leftover cooked cauliflower: Choose a large onion to give more flavour. Cook with the other ingredients; add the diced cauliflower and milk and proceed as the basic recipe.
Use other vegetables: Choose broccoli, Brussels sprouts, celery, spinach. Allow 100 g/4 oz. Follow basic recipe or variations above.

NUTRITIONAL VALUE: If the vegetables are lightly cooked they retain their vitamin value.

LIGHT SOUPS

The following are ideal if followed by a sustaining main course.

AVGOLEMONO SOUP

450 ml/¾ pint chicken stock (see page 48)
25 g/1 oz brown or white long grain rice
2 egg yolks or 1 whole egg
1–2 tablespoons lemon juice, depending upon personal taste.

Pour the stock into a saucepan, bring just to boiling point. Add the rice and cook for 20 to 25 minutes, or until really tender. While the rice is cooking whisk the egg yolks or egg with the lemon juice in a basin. Place the basin over a saucepan of hot, but not boiling, water and whisk briskly until thick and creamy.

Lower the heat under the pan of stock and rice so the liquid no longer boils. Whisk in the egg and lemon mixture, heat for 1 minute without boiling.

MICROWAVE: Cook the rice in the liquid, as described on page 98, add the egg and lemon and heat for 15 seconds on Full Power.
NUTRITIONAL VALUE: A low calorie soup.

LEEK CONSOMMÉ

1 small onion, peeled and left whole
small bunch parsley
600 ml/1 pint chicken stock or consommé
175 g/6 oz leeks, very thinly sliced
salt and pepper

Heat the onion and parsley in the stock or consommé for 5 minutes. Add any green part from the leeks, cook for 3 to 4 minutes, then add the white part and continue cooking for 5 minutes. Do not allow the leeks to become too soft. Remove the onion and parsley. Add seasoning to taste.

VARIATIONS:
Use very thinly sliced and peeled cucumber or courgettes in the same recipe.

NUTRITIONAL VALUE: A low calorie soup.

NOTE: Ideally you should use a good home-made chicken stock (see page 64) in this soup. If substituting a stock cube use only half.

SAVOURY OAT SOUP

15 g/½ oz margarine
2 medium onions, finely chopped or grated
1 garlic clove, chopped
150 ml/¼ pint milk
300 ml/½ pint water
25 g/1 oz rolled oats
salt and pepper
½–1 teaspoon French mustard, or to taste
1 or 2 carrots, coarsely grated
1 tablespoon chopped parsley

Heat the margarine in a saucepan; add the onions and garlic and turn in the margarine. Pour the milk and water into the pan; bring just to boiling point. Sprinkle in the rolled oats; stir as the liquid comes to the boil, lower the heat, add the salt, pepper and mustard. Cover the pan and simmer for 10 minutes, stirring from time to time. Add the carrot(s) and parsley. Cook for a further 5 to 10 minutes.

MICROWAVE: This soup cooks well in a microwave cooker (see page 22) but takes the same cooking time.
NUTRITIONAL VALUE: A light, but satisfying soup, with some fibre.

SERVE HOT OR COLD

Cold soups have never been as popular as they should be, for they are wonderfully refreshing, as well as being satisfying.

As Mulligatawny Soup entails quite an amount of preparation the quantities given provide 4 good portions. The soup could be eaten hot one day and then served chilled the next. You could, of course, freeze any left after the first meal.

Garlic is given as an ingredient in this soup. If you do not use the herb frequently, it is a good idea to buy a bottle of garlic juice and add just a few drops instead of the clove(s) of garlic.

MULLIGATAWNY SOUP

25 g/1 oz margarine or 1 tablespoon oil
2 medium onions, finely chopped or grated
1 or 2 garlic cloves, chopped
1 small dessert apple, peeled and grated
1–2 teaspoons curry powder, or to taste
1.2 litres/2 pints lamb stock (see page 55) or
    chicken stock
2 medium carrots, grated
2 tablespoons desiccated coconut or 25 g/
    1 oz creamed coconut*
2 tablespoons sultanas
2 teaspoons sweet chutney
salt and pepper
½–1 tablespoon lemon juice
2 level teaspoons cornflour (optional)
*obtainable in packets: store in the
    refrigerator

Heat the margarine or oil in a saucepan, add the onions, garlic, apple and curry powder. Cook for several minutes. Add the stock. Bring to the boil, add the carrots and the rest of the ingredients except the cornflour. Cook for 15 minutes or until the vegetables are tender. The soup can be served like this or sieved or liquidized. If too thin, blend the cornflour with a little water, add to the soup or purée and reheat.
Serves 4

VARIATION:
Cold Mulligatawny: Sieve or liquidize the soup then chill well. Top with natural yogurt then with pieces of cucumber and tomato, or red and green pepper.

MICROWAVE: The soup can be cooked on **Full Power**. Allow only 1 litre/1¾ pints stock. Cooking time is very similar.
NUTRITIONAL VALUE: Although the soup adds little food value it is a good choice for a relatively low calorie dish.

FRUIT SOUP

225 g/8 oz soft berry fruits, such as
    raspberries
300 ml/½ pint skimmed milk
2 teaspoons sugar or honey

Sieve the fruit then whisk briskly with the milk and sugar or honey. If preferred, you can liquidize the fruit with the milk, sugar or honey. This does not necessarily get rid of all the pips. Serve ice cold or heat gently without boiling.

VARIATIONS:
Use 300 ml/½ pint purée made from cooked or ripe dessert apricots, apples, plums, etc.
To give a sharpness to the fruit add a little lemon juice, or use a good pinch of ground cinnamon to give extra flavour.
To enhance the food value use 450 ml/¾ pint milk. Cook 25 g/1 oz rolled oats in this, then add the fruit.

Mulligatawny soup (top) and Fruit soup (recipes this page)

COLD AND REFRESHING

The following soups are ideal for a main meal or supper dish in hot weather.

AVOCADO SOUP

Halve a large avocado, remove the stone and skin the fruit. Mash or liquidize with 1 tablespoon lemon juice, 300 ml/½ pint milk, 150 ml/¼ pint natural yogurt or 100g/ 4 oz fromage frais; season well. You could add a few drops of Tabasco sauce.

NUTRITIONAL VALUE: Less low caloried than some soups but almost a complete meal in itself.

CUCUMBER AND MINT SOUP

½ medium cucumber, peeled and chopped
2 tablespoons chopped spring onions
few mint leaves
300 ml/½ pint chicken stock or water
salt and pepper
150 ml/¼ pint natural yogurt
½ tablespoon lemon juice, or to taste
To garnish:
1 teaspoon chopped mint
1 tomato, skinned and finely chopped

Put the cucumber, onions, mint and chicken stock or water into a saucepan, add a very little seasoning. Cover the pan and simmer for 10 minutes. Sieve or liquidize. Allow to cool then blend in the yogurt, lemon juice and any extra seasoning required. Garnish with mint and tomato. Serves 2–3.

VARIATION:
Use 225 g/8 oz peeled courgettes instead of the cucumber and chives instead of mint.

FREEZING: The soup freezes well. Add the yogurt after defrosting.
MICROWAVE: Cook the cucumber etc. on **Full Power**. Allow approx. 8 minutes.
NUTRITIONAL VALUE: a low calorie and low fat soup.

SPEEDY GAZPACHO

300 ml/½ pint tomato juice
¼ small cucumber, peeled and finely diced
½ green pepper, seeded and diced
6–8 spring onions, finely chopped
½ tablespoon lemon juice
salt and pepper
2 tablespoons soft breadcrumbs

Blend the tomato juice with all the other ingredients. Chill well.

VARIATION:
Use chicken stock instead of tomato juice. Sieve or liquidize 2 or 3 ripe tomatoes, add to the chicken stock with the other ingredients and chill.

CLASSIC GAZPACHO

If sieving the mixture chop 700 g/1½ lb tomatoes; if liquidizing skin and chop.

Put the tomatoes through a sieve or liquidize with 2 chopped onions, ¼ diced cucumber and 1 or 2 chopped garlic cloves. Blend in 1 tablespoon olive oil, 1 tablespoon lemon juice and salt and pepper to taste. Chill well. Dilute with iced water. Serve with bowls of breadcrumbs, and diced cucumber, onion and green pepper. Serves 4

NOTE: The amount of oil is small in this version of Gazpacho to keep it low calorie.

FISH DISHES

Fish is a delicious food and an ideal choice as one gets older, for it is easily digested and an excellent source of protein. Most fish is relatively low in Kcalories and white fish is low in fat, too. While oily fish, such as herrings, mackerel, salmon and tuna have a relatively high fat content, this is not *saturated fat*, the importance of which is explained on page 128. Shellfish, with the exception of lobster and scampi, are high in cholesterol, so should not be eaten if you have been advised to follow a low-cholesterol diet. There are more details about this important regime on page 128.

Many people would claim that frying is *the* ideal way of cooking fish; it certainly is the most popular. The crisp coating on the outside 'seals in' the flavour of the fish and *perfectly* fried fish is a very pleasant dish. If you are anxious to avoid fried foods it is possible to achieve a similar result with the use of little fat (see page 36).

Inexpensive fish is just as nourishing as the more expensive varieties. Do not hesitate to try some of the less well-known varieties of fish you may find on sale.

There are many delicious ways in which to cook and serve fish of all kinds. If you have changed your diet, to eat more fish and less meat, you may feel that fish dishes are less satisfying and have less flavour. In this section you will find simple fish dishes but also a selection of recipes in which the fish is combined with a variety of other ingredients to give extra flavour and to make the dish really sustaining.

Using frozen fish

Most recipes in this book are suitable for frozen, as well as fresh, fish. It is advisable to buy the frozen product if you are not able to purchase *really* fresh fish. In some recipes it is recommended that the flesh is defrosted before preparing the dish. This is to allow the various flavours used to be absorbed by the fish or to make sure the coating will adhere to the flesh.

Where no mention is made of defrosting the fish it is quite satisfactory to use it in the frozen state.

To defrost frozen fish in the microwave cooker, follow the directions on the packet. If there are no instructions, place the fish portions on a flat plate and cover. Two fairly small portions of fish take approximately 5 minutes on the **Defrost** setting to thaw out. Drain and dry the fish then proceed as the recipe. If you have no microwave you can hasten the defrosting process by putting the packet of fish in cold – never hot – water.

Using oil to cook fish

In many of the dishes oil is an excellent fat in which to cook fish. In some recipes a specific oil is mentioned; this is because the particular flavour is ideal for that recipe. You could, of course, substitute any oil you prefer or use other types of fat. Oils and fats, such as margarine, are either polyunsaturated or saturated, so your choice may be governed by this fact. More details are on pages 128 and 130.

Microwave cooking of fish

As most of the fish dishes in this section can be cooked in the microwave there will be no specific instructions under each recipe unless there are points of particular importance to be made.

Nutritional value of fish dishes

As all fish is extremely nutritious there will be no specific points under each recipe unless of particular interest.

WISE FRYING OF FISH

If you enjoy fried fish, but are anxious to avoid adding too much fat to your meals, there are several ways in which you can minimise the amount used in frying.

Your choice of pan is important. A silicone coated (non-stick) pan means you can use about half the usual amount of oil or fat. A heavy frying pan can be preheated before you put in the oil or fat and this means once again you will need only about half the amount given in the recipe on this page. Be very careful as you add the oil or fat to the very hot pan.

The recipe for shallow frying is given, for smaller families rarely use a deep fryer. If you deep fry correctly less fat is absorbed by the food.

Coating the fish
It is usual to coat fish for shallow frying with flour (this can be lightly seasoned or flavoured with grated lemon rind or chopped fresh herbs or a little dried herbs). If you then use egg white, rather than whole egg, you have a successful base for the crumbs and save fat and calories from the egg yolk.

Choosing the oil or fat for frying
Oils labelled 'frying oils' are generally a blend of different types, these give good results in frying, but are not necessarily polyunsaturated (see page 128). Successful frying means getting the fat very hot before the fish is put into the pan. Butter or margarine tends to burn easily so oil, or special frying fat, are better for this particular method of cooking.

Draining the fish
Always drain the fried fish on absorbent kitchen paper for ½ minute before serving.

FRIED FISH

2 portions of fresh or frozen white fish
1 level tablespoon plain flour
½ egg or 1 egg white, lightly beaten
2 or 3 tablespoons crisp breadcrumbs,
*   depending on size of fish portions*
2 tablespoons oil or 50 g/2 oz frying fat
To garnish:
parsley
lemon wedges

Dry the fish well; frozen fish should be allowed to thaw out sufficiently for the coating to adhere well. Do not allow the small blocks of fish to become too soft for they are then inclined to break.

Dust the portions of fish with the flour then the beaten egg or egg white and finally with the breadcrumbs. Press these firmly against the fish with a palette knife before frying; chill if time permits.

While it is better to have a frying pan large enough to fry the two portions of fish together, do not use too large a pan, for this gives less depth of oil, or fat. Heat the oil or fat until a cube of bread dropped into this turns golden in 1 minute. Add the fish, fry steadily for 2 minutes, then turn over and fry for 2 minutes on the second side.

Thin fillets of fish may need another 1 minute cooking on a lower heat; thicker portions need 3 to 5 minutes. The fish is cooked when it becomes milky-looking, i.e. opaque. To check this, insert the tip of a knife into the thickest part of the fish.

Remove the fish from the pan; drain on absorbent kitchen paper. Add the garnish.

NOTE: Oven 'fried' fish, on page 38, is a very low fat recipe.

Speedy plaice Mornay (top – recipe page 38) and Trout in paprika sauce (recipe page 39)

USING THE OVEN FOR 'FRYING'

It is possible to achieve the effect of frying by coating the fish and baking it in a really hot oven. The oven and the baking tray must be preheated; if you feel the fish might stick to the tray, oil a piece of foil and preheat this on a baking tray. In view of the high oven temperature do not try to cook too large portions; they would scorch.

OVEN 'FRIED' FISH

2 portions of fresh or frozen white fish or
small whole fish
1 or 2 teaspoons lemon juice (optional)
salt and pepper (optional)
3 teaspoons oil
2–3 tablespoons crisp breadcrumbs
To garnish:
parsley
lemon wedges

Dry the fish well. Frozen fish should be defrosted sufficiently for the coating to adhere well.

You can flavour the fish with a little lemon juice and seasoning but this is not essential. Brush the fish on all sides with 2 teaspoons of the oil. This is a better coating than egg when oven 'frying' for it helps to keep the fish moist.

Meanwhile preheat the oven to hot (220°C, 425°F, Gas Mark 7); brush the remaining oil over a flat baking tray. Put in the oven to become really hot then place the coated fish on the hot tray.

Cook thin fillets of fish for 12 to 15 minutes; thicker portions, or small whole fish, for 20 to 22 minutes. Do not turn the fish over during cooking. Do not drain the fish on kitchen paper. Serve garnished.

GRILLED FISH

Grilling is a healthy way of cooking fish. You can appreciate the real taste of the fish with little, if any, extra flavouring, although this can be added if desired.

It is important to keep the fish moist; brush with melted butter or margarine (which can be flavoured with chopped herbs or lemon juice) before, and during, cooking. Lemon or orange juice, tomato juice, milk or wine could replace the fat.

Preheat the grill before placing the fish under the heat. Thin portions of fish can be placed on the grid of the grill pan, rather than in the grill pan itself. It is a good idea to put oiled foil under the fish; this makes washing-up easier and prevents the fish sticking to the metal grid.

SPEEDY PLAICE MORNAY

2 teaspoons oil or melted margarine
2 plaice fillets
1 teaspoon lemon juice
4 tablespoons natural yogurt
3 tablespoons finely grated cheese

Line the grill pan with foil; brush with half the oil or margarine to prevent the fish sticking to the foil. Lay the fillets over the foil; brush the remaining oil or margarine over the fish then sprinkle with the lemon juice.

Preheat the grill, cook the fish for 6 to 7 minutes or until almost tender. Coat with the yogurt and then the cheese. Return to the heat and cook for 2 minutes, or until golden brown.

VARIATION:
Any white fish can be used in this dish. If cooking thicker cutlets you will need to cook the fish for 4 to 5 minutes on one side

then turn the cutlets over; brush with oil and sprinkle with lemon juice and cook on the second side for the same time before adding the yogurt and cheese.

MICROWAVE: Cook the fish until just tender on **Full Power**; allow only 30 seconds after topping with yogurt and cheese.
NUTRITIONAL VALUE: An exceptionally low calorie dish, especially if low fat cheese is used.

MARINATED GRILLED PLAICE

2 thick fillets of plaice

For the marinade:
2 tablespoons white wine or dry cider
pinch garlic salt
pinch cayenne pepper
½ tablespoon lemon juice
1 teaspoon chopped tarragon or ½
  teaspoon dried tarragon
1 teaspoon chopped parsley
1 teaspoon corn or sunflower oil
To garnish:
2 tomatoes, thickly sliced
lemon slices

If the plaice is frozen allow it to defrost. Dry the fish well. Blend the ingredients for the marinade in a long shallow dish. Put the plaice in the marinade and leave for 1 hour then lift out of the marinade.

Line the grill pan with foil, place the fish on the foil and baste with the marinade. Preheat the grill. Cook the fish under the grill for approximately 6 minutes, or until just tender, basting once or twice with any marinade left. Arrange the tomato slices neatly on the fish and grill for 1 or 2 minutes. Serve garnished with lemon slices.

VARIATION:
Any white fish could be used; thick cutlets or portions of fish should be grilled for 5 minutes then turned over, basted with the marinade and cooked for the same time on the second side.

NUTRITIONAL VALUE: This dish is low in fat; the marinade keeps the fish moist during cooking.

TROUT IN PAPRIKA SAUCE

2 fresh trout or defrosted frozen trout
2 large tomatoes, sliced
salt and pepper
1 tablespoon plain flour
2 teaspoons corn or soya oil
1 garlic clove, halved
For the topping:
150 ml/¼ pint natural yogurt
½ teaspoon paprika
2 teaspoons chopped parsley
1 tablespoon chopped chives or spring
  onions

Slit the trout and remove the backbones, as described on page 107. Fill the fish with the sliced tomatoes. Blend the seasoning with the flour and coat the fish with this. Heat the oil with the garlic, add the trout and cook for 2 minutes on either side. Remove the fish from the frying pan and arrange in an ovenproof dish.

Blend the ingredients for the topping together. Spoon over the trout, covering the fish completely. Cover the dish and bake for 15 to 20 minutes in the centre of a preheated moderate oven (180°C, 350°F, Gas Mark 4).

To grill the fish: Do not use flour, brush with the oil, place in the grill pan or in a flameproof dish. Cook as timing for frying, then finish cooking in the oven.

BAKING FISH

Baking is suitable for most kinds of fish. The most important point to remember is that fish dries easily, so that a certain amount of fat or liquid should be used in the container. The fish and dish can be brushed with melted butter or margarine. You can bake the fish in milk or wine or cider or water flavoured with a little lemon juice. You could use tomato juice or tomato purée or sandwich the fish between sliced tomatoes and sliced cucumber.

Unless the recipe states otherwise, preheat the oven to moderately hot (190°C, 375°F, Gas Mark 5). Allow about 15 minutes for thin fillets; 20–25 minutes for thicker portions and 30–35 minutes for whole fish like codling or fresh haddock.

The method of cooking in foil given on this page is ideal for all the flavour of the food is retained.

COD NIÇOISE

½ teaspoon corn or soya oil
2 large ripe tomatoes, cut in thin rings
2 tablespoons finely chopped chives or
*   spring onions*
1 garlic clove, crushed or pinch garlic salt
salt and pepper
2 fresh cod steaks or portions of cod fillet or
*   frozen cod portions*
1 teaspoon lemon juice

Cut 2 squares of foil sufficiently large to wrap round the fish, brush with the oil. Put half the tomato slices with half the chives or spring onions, garlic or garlic salt and seasoning in the centre of the 2 pieces of foil. Add the fish, then sprinkle with the lemon juice. Top with the remaining ingredients, tomato slices last.

Fold the foil around the fish and other ingredients. Place the 2 foil parcels on to an ovenproof dish, in case any of the liquid runs out. Bake for 25 to 30 minutes in a preheated moderately hot oven (200°C, 400°F, Gas Mark 6). Open the foil with great care as the steam will escape.

VARIATIONS:
Add a few sliced green or black olives to give the true flavour of Provence.
For a more moist dish, pour 1 tablespoon white wine or dry cider over the fish before adding the topping.

ANDALUSIAN FISH

½ teaspoon oil
1 teaspoon finely grated lemon rind
2 cod steaks or portions of other white fish
*   or portions of frozen fish*
1 tablespoon lemon juice
2 large tomatoes, sliced
4 tablespoons finely chopped spring
*   onions or shallots*
½ green pepper, deseeded and diced
4 tablespoons peeled diced cucumber
salt and pepper

Cut 2 squares of foil and brush with oil, as described in Cod Niçoise (left). Press the lemon rind into the fish and sprinkle with the lemon juice. Put half the tomato slices, with half the spring onions or shallots, half the green pepper and 2 tablespoons cucumber on the pieces of foil. Add the lemon flavoured fish and season lightly. Top with the remaining spring onions or shallots, green pepper, cucumber and then the tomato slices. Fold the foil around the fish and other ingredients and proceed as Cod Niçoise.

Andalusian fish (top) and Cod Niçoise (recipes this page)

40

INEXPENSIVE FISH DISHES

Inexpensive coley or hake or other cheaper white fish could be used in any of the recipes on this, and the next, page.

The Fish Pie and Fish Crumble make excellent supper dishes, as they can be prepared ahead and heated as, and when, required. There are other fish dishes under Supper Dishes, pages 94 and 95.

COD AND MUSHROOM COBBLER

300 ml/½ pint milk
salt and pepper
225–275 g/8–10 oz cod fillet, or use other
  white fish
50 g/2 oz mushrooms, sliced
15 g/½ oz flour
15 g/½ oz margarine or low fat spread
½ tablespoon chopped parsley
For the cobbler topping:
100 g/4 oz self-raising flour or plain flour
  sifted with 1 teaspoon baking powder
25 g/1 oz margarine
½ tablespoon chopped parsley
1 teaspoon finely grated lemon rind
approximately 4 tablespoons milk

Pour the milk into a deep frying pan or a saucepan, add a little salt and pepper and the cod. Poach steadily for 10 minutes or until the fish is just tender. The milk will have evaporated during cooking until approximately 225 ml/7½ fl oz. Lift the fish from the liquid and break into fairly large flakes. Put into a 900 ml/1½ pint pie dish or casserole with the mushrooms.

Blend the flour with the margarine or low fat spread with a fork then add to the hot milk in the pan. Whisk or stir until a thickened sauce. Add the parsley and pour over the fish and mushrooms. Cover the container with foil or a lid and place in the oven, which should be preheated to moderately hot (200°C, 400°F, Gas Mark 6). Heat for 7 to 8 minutes. This stage is important for the topping must be put on to a well-heated base.

Add a good pinch of salt and shake of pepper to the flour, or flour and baking powder. Rub in the margarine then blend in the parsley and half the lemon rind. Add sufficient milk to make a soft rolling consistency. Press out the dough with your hands or with a rolling pin until 1.5 cm/½ inch in thickness. Cut into 4–6 triangles.

Remove the cover from the dish. Arrange the triangles over the fish mixture. Top these with the remaining lemon rind. Return the dish to the oven, uncovered. Bake for 15 minutes. Serve hot.
Serves 2 to 3.

VARIATIONS:
This is an excellent basic fish dish. Cooked peas and carrots or other vegetables can be added to the fish.
The cobbler topping can be topped with a little milk and grated cheese before it is baked.
Fish and Tomato Cobbler: The fish can be poached in tomato juice instead of milk, or in a tomato purée made by heating 2 or 3 skinned and finely chopped tomatoes with 150 ml/¼ pint water or white wine before adding the fish. If making the purée there is no need to thicken this with the flour and fat after cooking the fish.

NUTRITIONAL VALUE: A fish dish high in protein. The cobbler topping is easier to prepare than pastry and has less fat content. If you use wholemeal flour in the cobbler you add fibre to the meal.

FISH PIE

300 ml/½ pint White sauce (see page 75)
300 g/10 oz cooked white or oily or shellfish
  or a mixture of fish
salt and pepper and extra flavouring
225 g/8 oz mashed potatoes
15 g/½ oz margarine, melted

Blend the sauce with the flaked or diced fish. Season and add chopped herbs, diced cooked vegetables or diced raw fennel or tomatoes or mushrooms. Spoon into a 900 ml/1½ pint pie dish. Top with the potatoes and melted margarine. Put into a preheated moderate oven (180°C, 350°F, Gas Mark 4) and bake for 30 to 35 minutes.

FISH CRUMBLE

White sauce (see page 75), made with 25g/
  1 oz margarine, 25 g/1 oz plain flour, 225
  ml/7½ fl oz milk
225 g/8 oz cooked or canned fish, flaked
100 g/4 oz cooked vegetables, diced
salt and pepper and other flavourings
For the crumble topping:
100 g/4 oz plain flour
salt and pepper
other flavourings (see method)
50 g/2 oz margarine or low fat spread

Mix the sauce, fish and vegetables, season to taste. You can add chopped herbs, diced uncooked tomatoes or mushrooms and cinammon or nutmeg or curry powder. Spoon into a 900 ml/½ pint pie dish.

Blend the flour and seasoning. Rub in the margarine or low fat spread – never use spread labelled 'very low fat'. You can add chopped herbs and 25 g/1 oz grated cheese. Sprinkle over the fish mixture. Bake for 30 to 35 minutes in a preheated moderate oven (180°C, 350°F, Gas Mark 4). Serve hot.

BAKED COD WITH MUSHROOMS

2 cutlets or portions of cod
2 teaspoons plain flour
salt and pepper
pinch ground coriander or dried fennel
40 g/1½ oz margarine
1 medium onion, cut into thin slices
100 g/4 oz mushrooms, thinly sliced
1 tablespoon chopped parsley
150 ml/¼ pint natural yogurt
2 tablespoons soft breadcrumbs

If using frozen cod allow this to defrost. Dry the fish on absorbent kitchen paper. Blend the flour with a little salt, pepper and coriander or fennel. Coat the fish with the flour. Heat 25 g/1 oz margarine in a frying pan; cook the onion for 5 minutes, then add the fish and fry for 2 minutes on either side. Remove the onion and fish then add the mushrooms to the pan and cook slowly for 5 minutes.

Spoon half the mushrooms and half the parsley into a shallow casserole. Top with the fish and onions and then the remaining mushrooms and parsley. Spoon the yogurt over the ingredients. Melt the remaining margarine, blend with the breadcrumbs and sprinkle over the yogurt. Bake for 25 minutes in a preheated hot oven (190°C, 375°F, Gas Mark 5).

Serve with jacket potatoes and a green vegetable.

VARIATION:
Any other white fish could be used.

NUTRITIONAL VALUE: As a fairly generous amount of margarine is used in this recipe it would be wise to choose polyunsaturated.

PLAICE IN MUSHROOM SAUCE

2 large or 4 small plaice fillets
150 ml/¼ pint white wine or water with ½
*   tablespoon lemon juice*
1 sprig parsley
few thyme leaves or pinch dried thyme
salt and pepper
25 g/1 oz butter or margarine
100 g/4 oz button mushrooms, sliced
2 teaspoons cornflour
¼ teaspoon paprika
150 ml/¼ pint milk
To garnish:
lemon slices
parsley

Put the fish into a shallow casserole with the wine or water and lemon juice. Add the herbs and a little salt and pepper. Cover with a lid or foil. Cook for 20 minutes in a preheated moderately hot oven (200°C, 400°F, Gas Mark 6) or until the fish is tender.

Heat the butter or margarine in a saucepan, add the mushrooms and cook gently for 5 minutes. Blend the cornflour and paprika with the milk. Add to the mushrooms, then stir over a moderate heat until the sauce has thickened.

Lift the fish from the liquid on to hot serving plates. Strain the liquid and add a little to the mushroom mixture. Heat gently, but do not allow to boil; add seasoning. Pour a little over the fish and the rest round it, then garnish.

FREEZING: Do not freeze the cooked fish but frozen fish could be used.
MICROWAVE: Use **Full Power** and allow approximately 10 minutes to cook the fish, and 5 minutes to cook the mushrooms and make the sauce.
NUTRITIONAL VALUE: A method of cooking fish without fat that retains its good flavour. The sauce uses a small amount of fat.

PLAICE ROULADES

For the stuffing:
1 egg
2 tablespoons peeled and chopped
*   cucumber*
1 tomato, skinned and chopped
1 tablespoon chopped chives or spring
*   onions*
½ teaspoon white wine vinegar or lemon
*   juice*
salt and pepper

2 plaice fillets, skinned if possible
4 tablespoons white wine or 3½
*   tablespoons water and ½ tablespoon*
*   lemon juice or white wine vinegar*

Hard-boil the egg then shell and chop this. Blend with the other ingredients for the stuffing. Spread the stuffing over the fillets of plaice and roll firmly. Secure the rolls with wooden cocktail sticks.

Put the fish into an ovenproof dish and add the wine or water and lemon juice or vinegar. Cover the dish and bake for 20 to 25 minutes in a moderately hot oven (190°C, 375°F, Gas Mark 5). Remove the cocktail sticks.

VARIATIONS:
Whiting fillet or thin portions of cod, haddock or coley could be used instead of plaice fillets.

NUTRITIONAL VALUE: This recipe illustrates that a stuffing does not need to be high in fat content.

Monkfish in ginger and coconut sauce (recipe page 47)

POACHED FISH

Do not imagine that poaching is a dull method of cooking fish; it is a way of cooking in which the flavour of the fish is well maintained. It is important that the liquid does not boil rapidly; it should be kept at simmering point. Too rapid cooking would overcook and break the outside of the fish before the centre is tender.

Fish can be poached in fish stock, made as the recipe for Fish pilau on page 47, or in water flavoured with a little white wine or lemon juice and/or herbs or in milk. Some or all of the liquid could be used to make a sauce to serve with the fish, as in the recipe below. Simmer thin fillets for 3 to 4 minutes and thicker portions for 7 to 8 minutes.

FISH FLORENTINE

175–225 g/6–8 oz spinach
salt and pepper
300 ml/½ pint milk
2 portions of white fish, fresh or frozen
1 bay leaf
1 sprig parsley
15 g/½ oz butter or margarine
15 g/½ oz flour

Cook the spinach, drain and season well. Pour the milk into a deep frying pan or good-sized saucepan. Add the fish, seasoning and herbs. Bring the milk to simmering point then cook until tender (see timing above). Frozen fish will take 2 or 3 minutes longer.

Spoon the spinach into a warmed oven-proof dish, top with the well-drained fish. Measure out 150 ml/¼ pint of the milk left from cooking the fish. Heat the butter or margarine, stir in the flour, add the milk. Whisk or stir until thickened. Spoon over the fish and spinach.

VARIATIONS:
If preparing the dish ahead, top the sauce with 2 or 3 tablespoons of crisp bread-crumbs and 15 g/½ oz melted butter or margarine. Preheat the oven to moderately hot (190°C, 375°F, Gas Mark 5) and cook the dish for 20 minutes or allow 4 to 5 minutes on Reheat setting in the microwave cooker.
Add 25 g/1 oz grated cheese or chopped parsley or watercress or fennel leaves to the sauce for extra flavour.

STEAMED FISH

When food is steamed it retains both texture and flavour extremely well. Steaming is an excellent way to cook the rather delicate types of fish like sole, plaice and whiting fillets. Rather more robust types of fish, such as cod, hake or halibut can be steamed, especially if additional flavour is added, as suggested below.

If you have a proper steamer place the fish on a piece of oiled foil or in a greased dish; add the flavouring. Cover and steam over a saucepan of steadily boiling water. You can put small portions of fish on a strong plate; cover this with a second plate and steam over the boiling water. Do make sure the plate is safely balanced and remove the lid or covering plate very carefully as the contents are very hot.

Cooking times are a few minutes longer than for poaching.

Flavourings for steamed fish
The small amount of butter or margarine or low fat spread used on the fish gives some flavour. You could add a spoonful or two of milk or natural yogurt or fromage frais or give a refreshing flavour with a purée made from fresh tomatoes or peeled cucumber.

FISH PILAU

450 ml/¾ pint fish stock (see below), or
   water plus 1 tablespoon lemon juice or
   cider vinegar
225 g/8 oz white fish, weight when skinned
   and boned
1½ tablespoons oil, preferably sunflower
1 medium onion, finely chopped or grated
75 g/3 oz long-grain brown or white rice
salt and pepper
½ red pepper, deseeded and diced
2 tablespoons chopped parsley
50 g/2 oz mushrooms, sliced or left whole

To make the fish stock: Simmer the bones,
skin and head of a fish in about 600 ml/
1 pint water for 15 to 20 minutes. You can
add various flavourings if desired, e.g. 1
bay leaf, a little white wine, a slice of lemon
plus a little salt and pepper. Strain the
liquid. This stock sounds a lot of bother but
it does give extra flavour to the dish.

Cut the fish into 2.5 cm/1 inch pieces.
Heat the oil in a large saucepan, add the
fish and turn in the oil for 2 or 3 minutes or
until delicately coloured. Remove with a
fish slice. Add the onion and the rice and
blend with any remaining oil.

Pour the fish stock or water and lemon
juice or vinegar into the saucepan, bring to
the boil and season to taste. Lower the heat.
Cover the pan and cook slowly for 15 to 20
minutes if using brown rice or 10 to 15
minutes with white rice. The rice should be
almost tender. Add the red pepper,
parsley, mushrooms and the diced fish.
Continue cooking for a further 10 minutes
or until all the ingredients are tender. The
Pilau should not be too dry.

VARIATIONS:
The recipe can be adapted in many ways.
Cook peas or diced carrots with the rice.

A true Pilau has 1 or 2 tablespoons pine
nuts added just before serving.

You could also add 1 or 2 tablespoons
sultanas or raisins to the rice mixture about
5 minutes before the end of the estimated
cooking time.

MONKFISH IN GINGER AND COCONUT SAUCE

1 tablespoon desiccated coconut
150 ml/¼ pint boiling water
1 tablespoon oil, preferably sunflower
1 small onion, finely chopped or grated
225 g/8 oz monkfish, cut into 2.5 cm/1 inch
   strips
salt and pepper
½–1 teaspoon ground ginger
½ tablespoon tomato purée

Put the coconut in a basin, add the boiling
water and allow to stand for 10 minutes.
Heat the oil in a frying pan or saucepan,
add the onion and cook gently for 5
minutes. Add the fish and cook in the oil
and onion mixture until slightly golden in
colour.

Blend a little salt and pepper with the
coconut and liquid, add the ginger and
tomato purée. Blend well then pour over
the fish. Cover the pan and simmer gently
for 10 to 12 minutes. Monkfish has a solid
texture and needs rather more cooking time
than many white fish.

Serve this dish with cooked rice.

VARIATIONS:
Use any other white fish in place of
monkfish.
If you like the flavour of coconut but do not
want the pieces of desiccated coconut in the
sauce, strain the liquid after the 10 minutes'
standing time and blend this with the other
ingredients.

MEAT DISHES

Many people consider that meat is *ideal* for a main dish, as it is full of flavour and is a very satisfying food. The excellent quality and variety of meats available enable one to choose wisely and cook practical dishes for all occasions. Why then, are we advised to eat less meat, especially as we get older?

All meats contain an appreciable amount of invisible, as well as visible, fat. These fats contain substances known as fatty acids, which over a period of time, tend to increase cholesterol levels in the blood. This is explained more fully on page 128.

The sensible approach, therefore, is to limit the amount of meat you eat. This can be done in two ways. You can have some days when meals are based upon fish, lean poultry such as chicken and turkey, and vegetarian dishes of all kinds as a change from meat. The other way to cut down on your intake of meat is to choose dishes in which a very limited amount of meat is augmented with an interesting variety of other foods.

Wise ways to cook meat

If you are following the recommendations above, and decide to eat meat less frequently, it is important that, on the occasions when you do serve meat, you preserve all its good flavour.

Do not be alarmed by the advice to use less fat in cooking; you will find that the modern approach enables you to enjoy the true flavour of the meat.

Choose meats critically, avoid fat cuts or cut away surplus fat. Ready-minced meat often has a large percentage of fat, so you may prefer to buy stewing steak and mince this at home.

Boiled meat is not dull; two of our best known recipes, given on page 55, are based on this method. You also have the bonus of stock to use in other dishes, or as a basis for interesting clear sauces.

Small portions of meat are not at their best roasted, so you may like to reserve this method of cooking for the times when you entertain friends. There are unusual casseroles too. These would be equally good for everyday fare. As the quantities given are for 4 people you can either reduce these or freeze any left over.

Good stock

In addition to the stock made by boiling meat or chicken (see pages 55 and 64), you can prepare stock by simmering the poultry carcass or meat bones in water to cover. Cook for about 1 hour. The stock could be prepared in a covered casserole in the oven when you are cooking other foods on a low heat. This saves fuel.

MICROWAVE: Use a large bowl or casserole. Bring the liquid just to the boil on **Full Power** then cook for 15 to 20 minutes on the **Simmer** setting.

To freeze stock

If you have no immediate use for the stock then freeze it in suitably sized containers or boil the liquid until very concentrated and pour it into ice-making trays. Freeze then remove the cubes of stock and pack. Use as and when required.

Clear sauces to serve with meat

Flavour the stock with tomato purée or with mushroom ketchup or sherry or red wine. Add chopped herbs to the stock. To make a creamy sauce blend equal quantities of natural yogurt and stock. Heat gently.

Stir-fried beef (top – recipe page 51) and Steak and pineapple kebabs (recipe page 50)

COOKING STEAK

If you have been in the habit of frying or grilling good quality steak with a generous amount of butter during the cooking process, you may be a little worried as to how you can reduce the fat used and still produce tender and moist steaks. The recipes that follow illustrate that the fat can be reduced with no adverse effect.

The first recipe uses moist fruit, to give flavour to the meat, plus a very small amount of fat.

STEAK AND PINEAPPLE KEBABS

2 rings of fresh pineapple about 2.5 cm/1 inch in thickness
175-225 g/6-8 oz fillet or rump steak
15 g/½ oz butter or margarine, melted or ½ tablespoon sunflower oil
1 tablespoon dry sherry

Cut away the peel from the pineapple; it is easier to do this with kitchen scissors rather than a knife. A surprising amount of juice flows from the fruit so remove the skin over a basin so the juice is not wasted. Cut out the hard centre core with an apple corer. Divide each pineapple ring into 4 to 6 segments.

Dice the steak into pieces slightly smaller than the pineapple pieces. Put the pineapple and steak on to 2 metal skewers. Blend the melted butter or margarine or the oil with the sherry and juice from the pineapple. Brush over the meat. Preheat the grill and cook the meat and pineapple for 4 to 8 minutes, depending how well cooked you like the steak.
NOTE: Pineapple juice tenderizes meat when the two are cooked together.

SPEEDY MEAT DISHES

The recipes that follow are ideal when you do not want to spend too much time cooking. Minute steaks are thin slices cut from the sirloin or rump. The term 'escalope' used to be used for thin slices of veal. Nowadays we can also buy escalopes of chicken, turkey, pork or lamb (cut from the top of the leg).

Minute steaks or escalopes are good when you want to eat less meat. It is possible to cook them with little fat.

STEAK DIANE

1 minute steak (see above)
15 g /½ oz butter or margarine
1 small onion or shallot, finely chopped or grated
salt and pepper
1 tablespoon chopped parsley
1–2 teaspoons Worcestershire sauce
½ tablespoon brandy or sherry (optional)

If the steak is a little thicker than you would like, flatten it with a rolling pin. Heat the butter or margarine and cook the onion or shallot for several minutes. Add the steak and cook for 1 minute on either side. Add the remaining ingredients, heat for a few seconds then serve.
Serves 1

VARIATION:
Steak au Poivre: Season the steak with a generous amount of black pepper or press crushed peppercorns into the meat on both sides. Fry the onion or shallot and meat as the recipe above. Stir 4 tablespoons natural yogurt over the meat plus 1 or 2 teaspoons of sherry or brandy or a few drops of Worcestershire sauce. Heat without boiling, or the sauce will curdle.

STIR-FRIED BEEF

175–225 g/6–8 oz rump steak or topside of
  beef, cut in a 2.5 cm/1 inch slice
For the marinade:
1 tablespoon oil
1 medium onion, finely chopped or grated
1 garlic clove, chopped or crushed
2 tablespoons cider or red wine or half stock
  and half vinegar

½ green pepper, deseeded
½ red pepper, deseeded
½ tablespoon oil
4 tablespoons chopped celery heart
few small cauliflower florets
1 teaspoon cornflour
4 tablespoons beef stock or water
1–2 teaspoons soy sauce
salt and pepper

Cut the beef into 5 cm/2 inch strips, about 2 cm/¾ inch in width. Mix together the ingredients for the marinade, put the beef in this and leave for 30 minutes. Cut the peppers into strips about half the length of the meat.

Heat the ½ tablespoon oil in a pan then cook the vegetables for 2 minutes, turning with a spoon throughout, so they cannot burn. Add the meat, plus the marinade and continue cooking for 3 to 5 minutes, depending on personal taste. Blend the cornflour with the stock, or water, and soy sauce, add to the meat mixture with a little seasoning. Stir over a moderate heat until the sauce has thickened.

VARIATIONS:

If you do not want to eat the slightly under-cooked onion and garlic in the marinade, lift out the meat then strain the marinade before adding it to the pan.

Use any selection of vegetables that you have available to make a complete meal.

STUFFED ESCALOPES

2 escalopes of veal, pork , chicken or turkey
For the stuffing:
1 lean bacon rasher, derinded and
  chopped
2 medium tomatoes, skinned and chopped
25 g/1 oz soft breadcrumbs
1 tablespoon chopped parsley
½ tablespoon lemon juice
salt and pepper
For the sauce:
1 medium tomato, skinned and finely
  chopped or 1 tablespoon tomato purée
2 tablespoons chopped spring onions or
  chives
1 tablespoon dry sherry
150 ml/¼ pint chicken stock

Beat the escalopes until very thin. Blend the ingredients for the stuffing together. Spoon over the pieces of meat. Roll firmly and secure with wooden cocktail sticks. Put into a casserole. Mix the sauce ingredients, pour over the meat; cover the casserole. Cook for 40 minutes in a moderate oven (180°C, 350°F, Gas Mark 4). Remove the cocktail sticks before serving.

VARIATION:

Stuffed Chicken Escalopes: Use the filling as above but omit the bacon in the stuffing and add 50 g/2 oz chopped mushrooms. Roll the escalopes firmly, then roll ½ to 1 bacon rasher around them. Secure with cocktail sticks. Fry for a few minutes to extract the surplus fat, then put into the casserole and proceed as above.

MICROWAVE: Cook for approximately 12 minutes on **Simmer** (50% of full output).
NUTRITIONAL VALUE: This makes a pleasant change from the familiar coated and fried escalopes. There is little fat in this dish, or in the sauce to serve with the meat.

51

A NEW LOOK TO LAMB CHOPS

Loin or chump lamb chops can be served in various ways. Allow a good-sized chop for each person. Try these easy dishes. Quantities are enough for 2 chops.

DEVILLED LAMB: Blend 2 teaspoons malt vinegar with 1 teaspoon oil, ½ teaspoon curry powder, a pinch dry mustard powder, 1 teaspoon tomato purée and a few drops of Worcestershire sauce. Brush some of the mixture over the chops. Cook under a preheated grill for 5 minutes, turn the chops and coat with the remaining mixture.

Continue cooking for a further 5 minutes, or until the chops are tender. Serve with cold natural yogurt. This can be flavoured with a pinch of curry powder and mustard powder.

ORCHARD LAMB: Marinate the chops in apple juice for 1 hour. Drain and grill as above. Core, but do not peel, a good-sized dessert apple and cut it into rings. Brush these with a few drops of oil and cook under the grill for about 5 minutes.

APRICOT-ORANGE LAMB

1 large orange
lamb or chicken stock or water (see method)
75 g/3 oz dried apricots, cut into strips
2 or 3 rosemary sprigs
1 tablespoon apricot jam
salt and pepper
4–6 lamb cutlets

Grate the rind from the orange. Squeeze out the juice and add enough stock or water to give 225 ml/7½ fl oz liquid. Mix the rind with all the other ingredients except the lamb. Leave for 1 hour. Cook the cutlets in their own fat in a frying pan until browned then add the apricot mixture. Cover the pan and cook gently for 10 minutes. Remove the rosemary before serving.

LAMB CUTLETS KORMA

4 small or 2 larger lean lamb cutlets
For the marinade:
1 medium onion, finely chopped or grated
1 garlic clove, crushed
½ tablespoon chopped fresh mint or 1 teaspoon dried mint
1 tablespoon lemon juice or white wine vinegar or white wine

1 tablespoon oil
150 ml/¼ pint lamb stock (see page 55), or chicken stock (see page 64)
pinch ground ginger
pinch saffron (optional)
pinch ground coriander
salt and pepper
5 tablespoons natural yogurt
25 g/1 oz seedless raisins

Put the cutlets in a dish, and add the marinade ingredients. Leave for about 1 hour, turning once or twice. Heat the oil, cook the cutlets and the rest of the marinade ingredients for 3 to 4 minutes, turn the meat and cook for the same time on the second side. Blend the stock with the ginger, saffron (if using this) and the coriander. Pour over the lamb, add a little salt and pepper. Cover the pan and simmer for 15 minutes. The liquid should have been reduced to about half by this time. Blend in the yogurt and the raisins. Heat without boiling and serve with cooked rice.

NUTRITIONAL VALUE: An excellent dish with only a small amount of fat.

Apricot-orange lamb (recipe this page), served with petits pois and baby onions

VERSATILE MINCED BEEF

The first recipe on this page gives a generous amount of beef for 4 people. It often saves cooking time to prepare a basic minced beef mixture then divide it and add different ingredients to each half. Follow this procedure and create many new and interesting dishes. The food should be eaten soon after cooking, or put in the freezer. Minced beef, whether cooked or uncooked, deteriorates quickly, due to the many cut surfaces. Each dish serves 2.

The basic minced beef mixture:
1½ tablespoons oil
2 medium onions, chopped or grated
450 g/1 lb minced beef
300 ml/½ pint beef stock
3 medium carrots, diced or grated
2 tablespoons tomato purée
salt and pepper
1 bay leaf
sprig of parsley

Heat the oil, add the onions and cook gently for 5 minutes. Stir in the beef and continue cooking until golden brown. Pour in the stock. Bring to the boil, stirring well to make sure the beef keeps quite smooth. Add the remaining ingredients. Cover the pan and simmer for 30 minutes. Halve the mixture. Remove the herbs.

Portion 1 – BEEF ITALIENNE
Add 2 tablespoons red wine, 1 crushed garlic clove or few drops garlic juice, 50 g/2 oz chopped mushrooms. Reheat in an uncovered pan for 15 minutes, stirring from time to time. Serve with pasta or rice or in pancakes.

Portion 2 – PAPRIKA BEEF
Blend 2 teaspoons sweet paprika with 150 ml/¼ pint stock or water. Add to the hot beef mixture with 2 skinned chopped tomatoes and 3 medium potatoes, cut into 2.5 cm/1 inch dice. Cover the pan, cook steadily for 15 minutes. Serve with a green vegetable.

SPEEDY BEEF STIFADO

½ tablespoon oil
225 g/8 oz onions, finely chopped or grated
1 or 2 garlic cloves (see method)
225 g/8 oz tomatoes, skinned and chopped
225 g/8 oz raw minced beef
1 tablespoon red wine vinegar or red wine
150 ml/¼ pint beef stock or water
salt and pepper

Heat the oil in a saucepan, add the onions and turn in the oil. If you are fond of garlic this can be crushed or chopped and cooked with the onions. If you like a more delicate flavour leave the garlic cloves whole and remove after cooking with the onions.

Add the tomatoes and beef and mix with the onions. Pour in the vinegar or wine and the stock or water. Bring the liquid to the boil, stirring frequently to make certain the minced beef is kept smooth. Add seasoning to taste. Cover the pan with a tightly fitting lid. Cook for 30 minutes.

VARIATION:
The traditional recipe for Beef Stifado is made with whole small onions or shallots and diced stewing steak. Turn the onions and garlic in the oil, add the tomatoes, beef, vinegar or wine. Increase the amount of stock or water to 300 ml/½ pint. Cook for 2 hours or until the beef is tender. Check the liquid is sufficient during cooking.

FREEZING: As this dish freezes well it is worthwhile cooking double.

BOILED MEATS

The recipes on this page for boiled meats are old traditional dishes. These lend themselves very well to cooking for smaller families. The beef left after the hot meal is excellent served cold with a salad. Most beef, and best cuts of lamb, are fairly lean nowadays; if you have been told to cut down on your fat intake cook the dish one day (do not overcook it), allow to cool then place in the refrigerator. Next day lift away the fat from the top of the liquid.

Always reheat boiled meat or poultry or casserole dishes very thoroughly.

BOILED BEEF

fresh or salted brisket or silverside of beef
vegetables to taste
salt and pepper (see method)

While fresh beef is better if you are trying to reduce the salt content in your diet, the salted beef has a better colour. If buying salted beef, soak it overnight in cold water to cover before using it.

Weigh the beef and put it into a saucepan with fresh water to cover completely. Add a few seasonal vegetables to flavour the meat. Bring the liquid to the boil. Add salt and pepper if cooking fresh beef, but pepper only with salted beef. Bring the liquid to the boil, cover the pan. Lower the heat and allow the liquid to simmer. Allow 30 minutes per 450 g/1 lb and 30 minutes over. Fresh vegetables can be added during cooking, so they retain their good flavour. Serve with mustard or a Mustard sauce (see page 75).

It is traditional to serve dumplings with this dish: see the recipe for Low-fat dumplings on page 130.

BOILED LAMB AND CAPER SAUCE

6 portions of neck of lamb (see method)
6 small onions or 2 larger onions, sliced
sprig of mint
salt and pepper
6 small carrots, left whole
For the sauce:
15 g/½ oz margarine or low fat spread
15 g/½ oz plain flour
150 ml/¼ pint lamb stock
4 tablespoons milk
1 teaspoon capers
few drops caper vinegar

It is usual to make this dish with cheaper cuts from the neck of lamb, or even from mutton, i.e. the scrag or middle neck. As these are cuts with a high fat content you may feel it wise to use the more tender and lean best end of neck of lamb. You can, of course, cut away the fat from the scrag or middle neck, in which case you may need to buy a larger quantity of meat.

Put the meat into a saucepan, add enough water to cover, then the onions, mint and a little seasoning. Cover the pan, bring the liquid to the boil, lower the heat and allow the liquid to simmer.

Best end chops take 45 minutes; less tender portions 1 to 1¼ hours. Add the carrots during the cooking period, so they retain a firm texture. Make the sauce, as White sauce (see page 75), using the stock and milk. When thickened, add the capers, vinegar from the caper jar and seasoning. Do not boil.

VARIATION:
Springtime Lamb: Cook the lamb with a selection of early young vegetables. The sauce can be flavoured with chopped mint instead of capers.

55

VARIETY MEATS

The Americans call liver, sweetbreads, kidney, etc. the 'variety meats' which somehow makes them sound much more enticing than the more familiar 'offal'.

Whatever the title, this group of meats can add a great deal of variety to the menu. Sadly, though, there is one drawback about buying these foods. All are relatively high in cholesterol, so if you have been advised to follow a low-cholesterol diet, you should very rarely serve them. This is a pity, for liver, in particular, is a highly nutritious food and a major source of iron.

If you are not on any special diet then eat them from time to time.

Cooking liver

Liver is a very lean meat and one that is spoiled by overcooking, even by one or two minutes, or by being kept hot before being served. It should be eaten as soon as it is cooked, so you enjoy the meat when it is moist and juicy, rather than being hard, dry and thoroughly unappetising, as it will be if it is overcooked.

Calf's liver is the more tender and has the more delicate flavour, but lamb's liver can be nearly as good if cooked carefully. It is appreciably less expensive.

The most popular ways to cook liver are to fry or grill it with bacon. If frying, cook the bacon rinds first to extract the fat then fry the liver in this with the bacon.

If grilling the liver keep this moist by basting it with bacon fat, oil or margarine.

Thin slices of liver cooked quickly by frying or grilling will be ready if cooked for about 1½ minutes on either side for people who like it 'pink' in the middle.

The dish on the right gives liver a new taste. You will find recipes for other variety meats on pages 138 and 143.

LIVER CASALINGA

salt and pepper
225 g/8 oz calf's or lamb's liver, cut into thin slices
1 tablespoon oil
2 medium onions, cut into thin slices then separated into rings
1 teaspoon finely chopped sage or ¼ teaspoon dried sage
6 tablespoons white wine or dry cider
2 tablespoons chopped parsley

Season the liver lightly, but do not use too much salt for this draws out the meat juices. Heat the oil and cook the liver for ½ minute on either side, then remove from the frying pan. Add the onions, sage and white wine or cider. Cover the pan and simmer gently for about 10 minutes, or until the onions are very tender.

Return the liver to the frying pan, stir to make sure this is well coated with the onions and any wine remaining. Add the parsley and continue cooking for about 3 to 5 minutes or until cooked to personal taste.

VARIATION:

Goujons of Liver: Cut the liver into small ribbons; season well, adding only a little salt but plenty of pepper and a little dry mustard powder. Cook as above, but add 1 or 2 tablespoons of tomato purée to the onions and wine when these are tender before returning the goujons to the pan.

MICROWAVE: If cooking tender liver in the microwave use the **Defrost** setting, rather than **Full Power**. Time carefully.
NUTRITIONAL VALUE: A relatively low fat way of cooking an important food.

Liver casalinga (top – recipe this page) and Beef Italienne (recipe page 54)

BASED ON COOKED MEAT AND POULTRY

Cooked meat or poultry, left over from cooking a joint or a whole bird, or the meat bought ready-cooked from a delicatessen counter, can provide the basis for a range of interesting main dishes.

Always make sure that the cooked meat is cooled well then stored carefully in the refrigerator and eaten within a day or two at the most. Keep all cooked meat or poultry well wrapped and away from uncooked meats of all kinds when in the refrigerator.

If you are reheating the cooked food make sure it reaches boiling point if heated in liquid or that the meat or poultry is very hot if heated by other means. This will destroy any harmful enzymes or bacteria.

The first three recipes that follow are unusual in that the basic dish can be adapted to be served hot or cold.

Freezing cooked meat and poultry
Never slice the food too thinly if it is to be frozen as slightly thicker slices retain the flavour and texture better.

If freezing a fairly large quantity of sliced meat freeze this on an open tray; as soon as the meat is frozen, pack with waxed or greaseproof paper between the slices. In this way you will be able to remove exactly the amount of meat you need for a particular meal.

Microwave reheating of cooked meats
It is ideal if you can reheat the cooked meat in its sauce etc. in the microwave cooker, rather than in a saucepan. The food, if correctly reheated, keeps its original fresh flavour. Use the Reheat setting and time the reheating very carefully.

SWEET AND SOUR LAMB

For the marinade:
2 teaspoons oil
3 teaspoons lemon juice or white wine or malt vinegar
1/4 teaspoon ground ginger
1/4 teaspoon ground cinnamon
2 teaspoons honey or brown sugar
salt and pepper

175-225 g/6-8 oz cooked lean lamb, diced
75 g/3 oz cooked brown or white long-grain rice
extra ingredients (see below)

Blend the marinade ingredients together. Add the lamb and leave for 1 hour.

To serve cold: Blend the marinade, lamb and cold rice together. Add 4 tablespoons diced celery, 1 sliced tomato, 1 or 2 grated raw carrots. Serve on a bed of lettuce or other green salad ingredients.

To serve hot: Heat together the marinade, lamb, 2 tablespoons chicken stock or water and the rice. Add 2 tablespoons seedless raisins plus 2 or 3 tablespoons diced red or green pepper.

HAM WITH GINGER AND APPLE SAUCE

2 dessert apples, cored and thinly sliced
150 ml/1/4 pint apple juice
150 ml/1/4 pint ginger ale
1 teaspoon arrowroot or cornflour
2 tablespoons apple or redcurrant jelly
1 or 2 pieces preserved ginger, chopped
175-225 g/6-8 oz cooked ham, sliced

Put the apples, apple juice and most of the ginger ale in a pan. Cover and simmer gently for 5 to 6 minutes, or until the apples are tender, but unbroken. Blend the arrowroot or cornflour with the remaining ginger ale. Add to the liquid in the pan with the jelly and ginger. Stir over a low heat until a smooth thickened sauce. Allow to cool.

To serve cold: Arrange the ham on the plates with a generous helping of the sauce.

To serve hot: Make sure the sauce is not too thick. If the liquid has evaporated too much in cooking add a little more juice or ginger ale or water. Place the ham in the very hot sauce; heat for 2 or 3 minutes. Serve with lightly cooked carrots.

VARIATION:
Cooked pork is equally good in this dish.

CHILLI BEEF

For the marinade:
1–2 teaspoons chilli powder or a few drops of Tabasco sauce
2 tablespoons red wine
1 garlic clove, crushed
4 tablespoons chopped spring onions
salt and pepper (see method)
1 teaspoon made mustard

225 g/8 oz cooked fresh or salted or corned beef, diced
1 red pepper, deseeded and diced
100 g/4 oz canned red kidney beans
extra ingredients as given in the method

NOTE: Chilli powder varies in strength, so add it gradually and taste the marinade.

Mix the marinade ingredients together, omitting the salt with salted or corned beef. Add the beef and leave for 30 minutes then blend with the red pepper and well-drained canned beans.

To serve cold: Stir in ½ tablespoon corn oil, a little chopped parsley and 1 or 2 sliced tomatoes. Serve on a bed of green salad.

To serve hot: Heat 150 ml/¼ pint beef stock with 2 tablespoons tomato purée or 2 skinned chopped tomatoes. Add the beef mixture and heat thoroughly. Serve with cooked vegetables.

VARIATIONS:
Cooked turkey or chicken leg meat are very good in this dish, as is cooked lamb.

CHICKEN À LA KING

For the sauce:
25 g/1 oz butter or margarine
50 g/2 oz mushrooms, sliced
15 g/½ oz plain flour
225 ml/7½ fl oz milk or a mixture of milk and chicken stock
salt and pepper

175-225 g/6-8 oz cooked chicken, diced
100 g/4 oz cooked or canned sweetcorn

Hard-boil the egg, shell it and chop the white and yolk separately. Heat the butter or margarine in a saucepan, add the mushrooms and cook for 2 or 3 minutes; add the flour and the milk or milk and stock. Stir as the liquid comes to the boil and thickens slightly. Add a little seasoning then the chicken and sweetcorn. Heat thoroughly, add the chopped egg white. Top each portion with the chopped egg yolk.

Serve as a light meal with hot toast or as a main meal with cooked potatoes and a green vegetable.

VARIATIONS:
Add cooked peas or other vegetables to the mixture.
Use the same basic recipe for cooked lamb, ham, turkey or veal.

POULTRY AND GAME

In the past chicken and turkey were often hailed as a special treat. Today they provide some of the most economical and easily available meats. You will find that people who are non meat-eaters often will eat, and enjoy, poultry.

To be able to buy portions of fresh or frozen chicken or turkey is invaluable for a person living alone, or for a small family. It means you can purchase just the right cuts for a special dish. It is a good idea to keep a few packs of frozen chicken in the freezer.

As chicken is so versatile there are many recipes in this book, some using cooked chicken (see pages 59, 66 and 96). Turkey would be equally as good in the recipes. You can of course buy ready-cooked chickens, which may be useful if you are short of time. It is considerably cheaper, though, to buy a chicken and cook it at home. *Always make absolutely certain that a frozen bird is completely defrosted* before roasting, boiling or steaming.

Both chicken and turkey are low in saturated fat. From the health point of view, therefore, they are highly recommended.

Rabbit has a more robust taste than chicken. It does, however, share the same virtues in that it is adaptable and a low fat food. If you are fond of young rabbit you can substitute it in some of the chicken dishes.

Quail is a rather surprising bird for there is a good amount of flesh on the bones. Recipes for using quail and pheasant, another good choice for a small family, are on pages 63 and 62.

PERFECT ROAST CHICKEN

A really well-cooked roast chicken should be golden brown on the outside with really tender moist flesh. If you live alone and are buying chicken for a single meal look for a spring chicken. A good-sized bird for 2 people would be from 1-1.3 kg/2¼-3 lb (weight ready for cooking). You would be able to enjoy a meal of hot chicken one day and have some left over for a second dish.

Stuffing gives the chicken more flavour and helps to keep the flesh moist. Two unusual stuffings are given on page 62. Put the stuffing at the neck end but not in the body cavity.

To make sure the breast of the chicken keeps moist brush it with a little melted butter or margarine before cooking and place foil lightly over the bird; remove this halfway through the cooking time. A high-domed covered roasting tin is an excellent investment. It keeps chicken or meat moist with little, if any, extra fat and allows the skin to brown.

Weigh the bird with the stuffing to calculate the cooking time.

You can roast a prime quality fresh bird in a hot oven (200-220°C, 400-425°F, Gas Mark 6-7). Allow 15 minutes per 450 g/1 lb and 15 minutes over.

A defrosted bird is better cooked at a lower setting (160-180°C, 325-350°F, Gas Mark 3-4). Allow 25 minutes per 450 g/1 lb and 25 minutes over.

Poultry varies in quality, so to check if it is cooked insert the tip of a knife or a skewer in the flesh where the leg joins the body. If no clear pink liquid runs out the bird is cooked.

Dijon rabbit (above left) and Basque chicken (recipes page 63)

STUFFINGS FOR CHICKEN

The following recipes give adequate portions for 4 people so for 2 people you can serve it hot one day and cold another. The stuffings are equally good hot or cold. They would be excellent with turkey too, or with rabbit or a game bird.

If you do not want to cook the stuffing at the neck end of the chicken, place it in a dish and cover tightly. Cook for 30 to 35 minutes in the hot oven, or 55 to 60 minutes at the lower setting (see page 60).

MICROWAVE COOKING: Each stuffing takes 5 minutes on **Full Power**; cook the onion first in the margarine for 2 minutes.
NUTRITIONAL VALUE: Both stuffings have fibre; the first recipe is particularly good.

LIVER AND OAT STUFFING

uncooked chicken liver, chopped
1 medium onion, finely chopped or grated
25 g/1 oz rolled oats
25 g/1 oz soft wholemeal breadcrumbs
25 g/1 oz margarine, melted
2 tablespoons chopped parsley
2 tablespoons milk
salt and pepper

Blend the ingredients together.

LEMON STUFFING

1 teaspoon grated lemon rind
50 g/2 oz breadcrumbs, white or brown
2 tablespoons lemon juice
2 tablespoons sultanas
25 g/1 oz margarine, melted
1 tablespoon chopped walnuts or hazelnuts
pepper

Blend the ingredients together.

ROASTING GAME BIRDS AND RABBIT

When choosing pheasant select a hen bird if possible; it may look smaller than the cock bird (easily distinguished by the spurs on its legs) but generally it has more flesh.

Pheasant is roasted in the same way as chicken. While it is not usual to stuff pheasant you could use the filling of cheese and grapes for quail, given on page 63, or one of the stuffings on this page.

Cover the bird with a little melted butter or margarine or with bacon rashers. A small pheasant takes about 1 hour in a preheated moderately hot oven (200°C, 400°F, Gas Mark 6). You can check to see if it is cooked in the same way as you test a chicken (see page 60). Pheasant, like other game birds, is generally served with game chips (potato crisps) and redcurrant jelly. Open the packet of potato crisps, spread these out on a flat tin; heat for 2 minutes.

A spring chicken, often called a poussin or broiler, can be cooked in the same way as the quail and so can really young pigeons (often called squabs).

Young rabbit can be roasted whole. Brush the flesh with a little oil or with melted margarine or cover with bacon rashers. Allow 15 minutes per 450 g/1 lb at 200°C, 400°F, Gas Mark 6 and another 15 minutes over.

Microwave roasting
A combination microwave cooker is ideal for roasting poultry, game birds and small joints. It takes less time, but results are the same as when a conventional oven is used.

An ordinary microwave cooker can be used; the flesh does not brown in the same way. Follow the instructions in the manufacturer's handbook as to the cooking and standing times.

QUAIL VERONIQUE

about 16 grapes, preferably seedless
50 g/2 oz curd cheese
2 large quail
25 g/1 oz butter, melted
To garnish:
lettuce heart
grapes, preferably seedless

If you can skin the grapes do so – this is quite easy if you pull the skin from the end where the grapes are attached to the stalk. If the grapes have seeds, slit them with the tip of a knife and use the knife to ease out the pips. Put the grapes and cheese into the bodies of the small birds. Brush the birds with the melted butter. Place in a roasting tin and cook for 40 minutes in a preheated moderately hot oven (200°C, 400°F, Gas Mark 6). Garnish with lettuce and unskinned but deseeded grapes.

DIJON RABBIT

2 joints of young rabbit
little oil or melted margarine
2 tablespoons Dijon mustard
4 tablespoons single cream or natural
   yogurt
salt and pepper

Brush the rabbit joints with the oil or margarine. Spread the mustard generously over the outside surfaces. Roast for 35 minutes in an oven preheated to moderately hot (200°C, 400°F, Gas Mark 6), or until tender. Remove from the roasting tin on to a heated dish and keep hot.

Add the cream or yogurt and seasoning to the juices in the roasting tin; season well. Heat, without boiling. Serve with the cooked rabbit.

BASQUE CHICKEN

25 g/1 oz margarine
1 or 2 bacon rashers, de-rinded and
   chopped
1 medium onion, finely chopped or grated
2 chicken portions
1 green pepper, deseeded and finely diced
2 tomatoes, skinned and chopped
150 ml/¼ pint white wine or cider or water
salt and pepper

Heat the margarine and bacon rinds in a deep frying pan or saucepan, add the onion and chicken portions and cook for 5 minutes. Remove the rind, put in the chopped bacon and cook for another 5 minutes. Add the remaining ingredients.

Cover the pan and cook for a further 10 to 15 minutes.

CHICKEN POACHED IN CIDER

2 chicken portions
salt and pepper
1 teaspoon paprika
25 g/1 oz margarine
300 ml/½ pint dry cider
100 g/4 oz very small button mushrooms
3 tablespoons natural yogurt or fromage
   frais (see page 130)
2 tablespoons chopped watercress leaves

Dust the chicken with salt, pepper and paprika. Heat the margarine in a deep frying pan or shallow saucepan. Add the chicken and turn in the hot fat for 5 to 6 minutes or until lightly browned. Add the cider and mushrooms. Cover the pan and simmer for 10 to 15 minutes. Remove the pan from the heat so the cider is no longer boiling. Add the yogurt or fromage frais and watercress. Heat, without boiling.

BOILED CHICKEN

This method of cooking chicken is ideal if you want to use the flesh for more than one meal since it is beautifully moist. The cooking liquid makes excellent stock.

1 chicken
2 onions, peeled
3 or 4 carrots
1 bay leaf
1 sprig parsley
salt and pepper

Defrost a frozen chicken before cooking. Put the bird into a good sized saucepan with water to cover. Add the onions, carrots, herbs and a little seasoning. Bring the liquid to the boil and then lower the heat and cover the saucepan. Allow the liquid to simmer gently.

When cooking a young chicken allow 15 minutes per 450 g/1 lb and 15 minutes over. NOTE: The giblets can be cooked with the bird; this makes a darker, less delicate-flavoured stock.

BRAISED CHICKEN

Place a selection of root vegetables at the bottom of the pan. These should be of a size that will become tender by the time the chicken is cooked but will keep their shape. You can add chopped celery and chopped herbs, like parsley, to give flavour. Add water or a mixture of water and wine to come halfway up the vegetables. Season lightly.

Place the chicken on top, checking that there is no surplus fat on it. Cover the pan with a *tightly fitting* lid. Cook as the timing for Steamed chicken, calculating this from the time the liquid comes to the boil. Check during the cooking period to see the liquid does not evaporate. Serve most of the vegetables with the chicken; sieve a few with the liquid to make a sauce.

You can use a deep casserole in the oven. For a 1 kg/2¼ lb chicken plus vegetables allow 1½ hours in a moderate oven (160°C, 325°F, Gas Mark 3).

STEAMED CHICKEN

This method of cooking chicken gives it a firmer texture than boiling. It is therefore better if you are preparing the chicken to have cold with salad. If you have a steamer sufficiently large to take the chicken place the bird in this. It is a good idea to keep the breast moist by covering it with lightly greased greaseproof paper.

The chicken flesh can be flavoured with a little lemon juice or with 1 tablespoon finely chopped parsley and 1 teaspoon finely chopped rosemary or fennel. Press the herbs firmly against the flesh.

Place the tightly covered steamer over a saucepan of boiling water. If you feel there is a problem about arranging the steamer over the heat, put it over the pan containing cold water then bring the water up to the boil as quickly as possible. Once the water boils allow 15 minutes per 450 g/1 lb and 15 minutes over cooking time.

If you do not possess a sufficiently large steamer then use a saucepan containing about 7.5 cm/3 inches of water only so that most of the chicken is above the liquid. Cook for the timing given above. The problem about this method is that you must remember to fill-up the saucepan with boiling water at regular intervals.

Braised chicken, cooked with a 'mirepoix' of vegetables (recipe this page)

CHICKEN IN CREAMED CURRY SAUCE

For the sauce:
2 teaspoons curry paste or curry powder or
    to taste
3 tablespoons mayonnaise
150 ml/¼ pint natural yogurt
2 tablespoons milk or chicken stock
2 portions cooked chicken
To garnish:
1 tomato, sliced
1 tablespoon desiccated coconut

It is advisable to heat the sauce in a basin over hot water. Curry paste gives a better flavour in this type of dish but curry powder can be used.

Blend the curry paste or powder with the mayonnaise, yogurt and milk or stock. Add the chicken portions and heat over a pan of boiling water for 10 to 15 minutes.

Garnish with the tomato and coconut.

CHICKEN-FRUIT CURRY

½ tablespoon oil
1 medium onion, finely chopped or grated
1 garlic clove, crushed
1–2 teaspoons curry powder, or to taste
½ teaspoon ground ginger, or to taste
2 chicken breasts, skinned and cut into
    5 cm/2 inch strips
1 dessert apple, peeled, cored and diced
300 ml/½ pint apple juice or half apple juice
    and half chicken stock
1 tablespoon sultanas
1 tablespoon desiccated coconut
salt and pepper

Heat the oil, add the onion and garlic and cook very gently for 5 minutes. Add the curry powder and ginger and then the rest of the ingredients. Cover the pan tightly.

Simmer for 20 minutes then lift the lid so the liquid evaporates slightly. Cook for a further 5 minutes. Stir once or twice during this time so the food cannot stick to the cooking pan.

MICROWAVE: An ideal dish to cook in the microwave cooker. As the quantity of oil is small do not reduce this amount but reduce the liquid to 225 ml/7½ fl oz.
NUTRITIONAL VALUE: An excellent way to give flavour to a low fat recipe.

FRIED CHICKEN SUPREME

1 tablespoon plain flour
salt and pepper
2 chicken breasts, skinned
25 g/1 oz butter or margarine
1 tablespoon corn or sesame seed oil

Blend the flour and seasoning. Coat the chicken with the flour, the quantity above gives a light dusting only. Heat the butter or margarine and oil. Fry the chicken briskly for 2 minutes, turn and fry for the same time on the second side.

Lower the heat and cook for a further 4 to 7 minutes, depending on the thickness of the flesh. Drain the chicken pieces on absorbent kitchen paper.

VARIATIONS:
If you have a non-stick pan use only the butter or margarine; omit the oil.
Chicken Escalopes: Flatten the chicken flesh to give a thin layer. Coat with the seasoned flour then beaten egg or egg white and finally with 2 to 3 tablespoons crisp breadcrumbs or rolled oats. Fry as before. Drain on absorbent kitchen paper before serving. Serve the Chicken escalopes with lemon slices.

GRILLED CHICKEN

Grilling is an excellent way to cook young chicken, provided the flesh is kept moist during the cooking period. This can be done by brushing the portions with a little melted butter, margarine or oil before and during cooking. The fat can be blended with a little lemon juice or chopped herbs, such as finely chopped rosemary or tarragon or a good pinch of dried herbs. Follow the timing given in the recipe below.

Instead of using fat of some kind to keep the chicken moist during grilling, you can marinate it before grilling.

To marinate 2 portions of chicken blend together:-
1 tablespoon lemon juice
1 teaspoon finely grated lemon rind
1 tablespoon finely chopped spring onions
  or chives
3 tablespoons chicken stock

Put the chicken portions into this mixture and leave for 30 minutes. Lift the chicken out of the marinade and grill for the same time as given in the recipe below. Spoon any marinade left over the chicken during cooking.

CHICKEN IN HONEY AND MUSTARD GLAZE

2 chicken portions, defrosted if frozen
1 teaspoon corn oil
½ tablespoon honey
15 g/½ oz butter, melted
1 or 2 teaspoons French mustard or
  made English mustard, amount
  according to taste.

Skin the chicken portions if possible, for the coating adheres better. Brush the chicken with the corn oil, then cook under a preheated grill for 10 to 12 minutes, or until nearly tender. Turn over once during this period. Blend the honey, butter and mustard together. Spread over the top surface of the chicken joints and return to the grill, lowering the heat slightly, so the mixture does not scorch, and cook for a further 5 minutes.

CHICKEN AND APPLE KEBABS

For the marinade:
4 tablespoons white wine or cider
1 tablespoon sunflower oil
1 teaspoon French mustard
pinch cayenne pepper

2 dessert apples
225 g/8 oz cooked chicken

Mix the marinade ingredients together. Cut the unpeeled apples into quarters; divide the chicken into cubes. Put the apples and chicken into the marinade; leave for 30 minutes. Line the grill pan with foil. Lift the chicken and apple slices from the marinade and put on to 2 long metal skewers, placing a piece of apple, then chicken, then apple until the skewers have been filled.

Preheat the grill and cook for 6 minutes, turning once. Baste with the marinade during the cooking time.

VARIATION:
Use uncooked, instead of cooked chicken and allow 10 minutes under the hot grill.

VEGETABLES AND SALADS

Vegetables form an important part of a well balanced meal; many are excellent used as the main ingredient to produce a complete and satisfying vegetarian dish.

Most vegetables are a first class source of mineral salts and vitamins. They also add important fibre to your meals. If you are anxious to avoid putting on weight it is reassuring to know that the majority of vegetables are low in fat and most have few Kcalories. Obviously, both the fat and Kcalorie content are affected by the way in which the vegetables are cooked.

Cooking a mixture of vegetables

When you are cooking for one or two people only, there may be a tendency to feel it really is too much trouble to cook a selection of vegetables as this means clearing up an undue number of pots and pans. With a little thought you would find you can cook different kinds of vegetables in the same saucepan. Choose those where the flavours blend well e.g. carrots with parsnips and peas; sliced courgettes or cauliflower florets with sliced leeks and sliced beans; potatoes, swede and carrots.

In some cases the cooking times will be identical; in others you will need to put the vegetable that needs the longest cooking time in the lightly salted water for a minute or two, then add the other vegetables.

Microwave cooking of vegetables.

This enables you to cook small quantities of different vegetables in individual covered bowls. Frozen vegetables are easier to cook well than fresh vegetables, as their size is uniform and they are young and tender.

Dual purpose vegetables

Certain vegetables can be bought in small quantities, so giving you enough for a particular meal. At other times you may find there is a possibility of some vegetable being wasted because you need to buy a whole lettuce or whole cabbage. A lettuce is very good cooked in the same way as other greens, or you could use it in the soup recipe on page 26 instead of the spinach.

You may have part of a cabbage heart or a few tender Brussels sprouts or young spinach leaves left after cooking a portion. The remainder can be used raw in salads. Cucumber is just as appetising when cooked as it is in a salad.

Naturally it is important to store vegetables in a cool place so they keep in perfect condition and are not wasted. The salad drawer of the refrigerator is ideal for keeping green vegetables.

Careful cooking of vegetables

If it is possible to keep the peel on potatoes do so; this adds flavour and fibre.

Do not prepare vegetables too far ahead as vitamins are lost if green vegetables are shredded and left standing or soaking in water. Prepare just before cooking.

Use the minimum of boiling water when cooking vegetables. You can flavour the liquid with chopped herbs, chopped onion, a little lemon juice or as the specific suggestion in the recipes. This means you need add little, if any, salt.

Steaming, rather than boiling, root vegetables retains both flavour and texture.

Cook vegetables lightly, they are so much better if they retain their fresh firm texture as well as their fresh flavour.

Courgette and tomato bake (top) and Vegetable jambalaya (recipes pages 70 and 71)

A NEW LOOK TO VEGETABLES

Green vegetables

Broccoli and cauliflower are delicious if a halved garlic clove and a little lemon juice are added to the water.

Add 1 or 2 chopped skinned tomatoes or a little tomato juice. This gives a new taste to cauliflower florets, shredded cabbage, Chinese leaves (Pak-choi) or Brussels sprouts.

Add a few sliced mushrooms and a very little chopped thyme when cooking spinach or cabbage.

Blend cooked cabbage or Brussels sprouts with lightly cooked dessert apple and onion slices or cook the apple and onion with the green vegetable.

Top Brussels sprouts with natural yogurt and blanched flaked almonds. These can be browned first.

Root vegetables

Young turnips, swedes and parsnips are delicious cooked and mashed with a generous amount of grated or ground nutmeg, chopped chives and a little margarine and natural yogurt.

You improve the flavour of older carrots if you add the juice of an orange in cooking.

For a piquant sweet-sharp taste add 1 tablespoon white wine vinegar together with 1 tablespoon sugar to the water in which you cook about 450 g/1 lb carrots.

Use more expensive vegetables, such as aubergines, for the main part of the dish.

COURGETTE AND TOMATO BAKE

175–225 g/6–8 oz courgettes
1 tablespoon corn or soya oil
350 g/12 oz ripe tomatoes, skinned and sliced
2 tablespoons finely chopped onions or chives
1 teaspoon chopped tarragon or ¼ teaspoon dried tarragon
salt and pepper
50 g/2 oz Cheddar or Edam cheese, finely grated
1 tablespoon white wine, cider or water

For the topping:
25 g/1 oz Cheddar or Edam cheese, finely grated
2 tablespoons soft breadcrumbs

Rinse the courgettes in cold water and dry well then cut into thin slices. Heat the oil and fry the vegetable slices for 1 minute on either side.

Place alternate layers of courgette and tomato slices in a 900 ml/1½ pint casserole, ending with a layer of tomatoes. Sprinkle the layers with the onions or chives, the tarragon, a little salt and pepper and the 50 g/2 oz of cheese. Add the wine, cider or water.

Blend the cheese and breadcrumbs for the topping. Spread evenly over the top layer of tomatoes and bake in a preheated moderate oven (180°C, 350°F, Gas Mark 4) for 25 minutes.

VARIATION:
Aubergine and Tomato Bake: Use 1 medium aubergine instead of courgettes. It can be scored lightly, sprinkled with salt and left for 30 minutes then rinsed in cold water. This draws out the bitter taste.

VEGETABLES MAKE A MEAL

There are many ways in which vegetables can form the main dish. Probably the most usual and popular are to served cooked vegetables with a cheese sauce (see page 75), or raw salads with cheese or hard boiled eggs.

The vegetables known as the 'pulses' are particularly important. They are excellent sources of both protein and fibre and can be used for a main meal without other proteins. Fresh or frozen beans and peas should be included frequently in your meal planning.

The dried pulses have the advantage of being inexpensive, fat free and satisfying. They can be used in many ways instead of meat. Make your favourite stew with cooked beans; use a variety of beans in a salad for hungry people (see page 106 for a good bean salad). Serve cooked pulses as an accompaniment to the light salads on page 74. Cooked dried beans, peas and lentils freeze well.

The recipes on this page and on page 72 mention using canned haricot and kidney beans. This is to save the bother of soaking and cooking the beans. You can, of course, substitute other cooked or canned beans. If cooking these you will need 150 g/5 oz dry beans instead of a 425 g/15 oz can, for these increase in weight almost threefold in the process of cooking.

To cook dried beans and dried peas
Soak the food in cold water to cover for 12 hours. Strain then put into a saucepan with fresh water to cover. You can add herbs, onions, tomatoes and seasoning.

The essential point about cooking these foods is that the water *should be brought to the boil and allowed to boil rapidly for 10 minutes.* This is essential as a safeguard against harmful bacteria.

After this time, cover the pan and boil steadily for the following times:–

Butter, haricot and kidney beans – 50 minutes. Soya beans and chick peas – 2 to 2¼ hours. Adzuki and flageolet beans and split peas – 30 minutes.

You can use either a microwave or pressure cooker. Consult the manufacturer's handbook.

VEGETABLE JAMBALAYA

1 tablespoon oil
2 medium onions, neatly diced
100 g/4 oz mushrooms, quartered
2 or 3 celery sticks, cut into 1.5 cm/½ inch pieces
½ small green pepper, deseeded and diced
1 × 225 g/8 oz can plum tomatoes
75 g/3 oz cooked brown or white long-grain rice
100 g/4 oz cooked or canned haricot beans
few drops Tabasco sauce or pinch chilli powder
salt and pepper

Heat the oil in a saucepan, add the onions, mushrooms, celery and pepper, turn in the oil and cook gently for 5 minutes. Add the tomatoes and the liquid from the can, the rice, beans, the Tabasco sauce or chilli powder. Heat together, stirring once or twice until well blended. Add seasoning.

MICROWAVE: Cook the vegetables in only ½ tablespoon oil in a covered bowl. Allow 3 to 4 minutes on **Full Power**. Add the remaining ingredients as in the recipe. Cover the container and heat for 4 to 5 minutes.
NUTRITIONAL VALUE: A vegetarian dish that provides high fibre plus protein.

STUFFED PEPPERS

1 red pepper
1 green pepper
15 g/½ oz butter or margarine
1 medium onion, finely chopped or grated
3 large tomatoes, skinned and chopped
50–75 g/2–3 oz soft breadcrumbs
1 tablespoon chopped parsley
50–75 g/2–3 oz Cheddar or other cheese, grated
salt and pepper

Halve the peppers lengthways. Remove the cores and seeds. Put the peppers into boiling water; cook for 4 minutes to soften. Drain and cool; place in an ovenproof dish. Heat the butter or margarine, add the onion; cook for 2 or 3 minutes. Blend with the tomatoes, just over half the crumbs, the parsley, half the cheese and seasoning. Press the mixture into the pepper halves, top with the remaining crumbs and cheese.

Bake for 20 minutes in a moderately hot oven (190°C, 375°F, Gas Mark 5).

MIXED VEGETABLE PÂTÉ

225 g/8 oz mixed vegetables (see method)
salt and pepper
For the sauce:
25 g/1 oz butter or margarine or low fat spread
25 g/1 oz plain flour
150 ml/¼ pint milk
1 tablespoon cream or natural yogurt
50 g/2 oz Cheddar or other cheese, grated

The vegetables should be as varied as possible. They will vary with the season but you could have a mixture of diced young carrots, diced peeled cucumber or courgettes, a few peas or diced green beans and finely diced celery. Cook for a few minutes in well seasoned water then strain. Do not allow them to get too soft, for they continue cooking to a degree as they cool.

Make a Cheese sauce as the recipe on page 75. Add the vegetables and put into a 600 ml/1 pint mould or tin. Cover with foil, so the top does not dry. Allow to cool.

SAVOURY BEAN LOAF

25 g/1 oz margarine
2 medium onions, finely chopped or grated
1 × 425 g/15 oz can red kidney beans
50 g/2 oz fresh wholemeal breadcrumbs
1 teaspoon chopped fresh sage or ½ teaspoon dried sage
50 g/2 oz cashew nuts or walnuts, chopped
1 tablespoon tomato purée
2 eggs
salt and pepper
few drops corn oil

Heat the margarine in a saucepan, add the onions and cook for 5 minutes. Remove from the heat. Drain the kidney beans; discard the liquid. Mix the beans with the onions in the saucepan then add the other ingredients and mix well. (The mixture may be briefly liquidized in a blender for a smoother loaf).

Grease a 900 g/2 lb loaf tin or line this with greased greaseproof paper. Spoon in the bean mixture and smooth flat. Cover the top of the tin with oiled foil. Bake in a moderate oven (180°C 350°F, Gas Mark 4) for 1 hour.

If serving hot: Cool for a few minutes and then turn out.

If serving cold: Place a plate then a weight on top and allow to cool in the tin.
Serves 4

Cheese and grape salad (left – recipe page 74) and Savoury bean loaf (recipe this page)

CHEESE AND GRAPE SALAD

225 g/8 oz cottage cheese
lettuce leaves
small portion cucumber, sliced
small bunch white grapes, deseeded
small bunch black grapes, deseeded
For the sauce:
1 tablespoon lemon juice
1 large ripe banana, sliced
2 tablespoons natural yogurt
salt and pepper
pinch sugar

NOTE: The easy way to remove grape seeds is by slitting the grapes with a small sharp knife and easing out the seeds. In this way the grapes remain whole.

Arrange the cheese on individual plates with the lettuce leaves, cucumber slices and grapes around the cheese.
    Blend the lemon juice with the banana and yogurt. Mash until smooth then add a little seasoning and the sugar. Spoon over the cheese.

ORANGE AND TOMATO SALAD

few lettuce leaves
2 medium tomatoes
2 tablespoons chopped chives or spring onions
salt and pepper
2 oranges

Arrange the lettuce on 2 flat plates. Cut the tomatoes into rings, arrange on the lettuce and top with the chives or spring onions and a very little seasoning. Cut away the peel from the oranges and cut the pulp into thin rings; do this over a basin so the juice is not wasted. Spoon this juice over the tomatoes and then arrange the orange slices on the plates. Serve well chilled.

APPLE, BACON AND SPINACH SALAD

For the mustard dressing:
1 teaspoon made English mustard or French mustard
2 teaspoons soya or sunflower seed or corn oil
1 tablespoon lemon juice or white wine vinegar
salt and pepper
1 teaspoon sugar

2 dessert apples
few very young spinach leaves
2 lean bacon rashers, de-rinded

Mix the ingredients for the dressing together. Core the apples, but do not peel them, and cut into thin wedges; put into the dressing. Wash the spinach leaves in cold water; dry well. Arrange on small plates or in salad bowls and top with the apples and dressing.
    Grill the bacon rashers until crisp; drain on absorbent kitchen paper to absorb surplus fat. Cut into pieces. Add the hot bacon to the salads and serve at once.

VARIATIONS:
Use a peeled and sliced avocado instead of the apples.
Choose other salad greens to use instead of spinach.

NUTRITIONAL VALUE: Spinach is an excellent source of iron and this is an ideal way to eat it. The spinach leaves must be young, tender and very fresh.

SAUCES

It is possible to make sauces with a low fat and low calorie content. The use of cornflour, rather than flour, reduces the calories. Use plain flour if possible.

Cornflour thickens easily. It is, of course, more expensive than flour.

Low fat spread can be used instead of butter or margarine. Polyunsaturated margarine is very satisfactory. Low fat spread should be used in the All-in-One method on this page. Never use spread marked 'very low fat' in cooking. It is suitable only for a spread on bread.

Skimmed or semi-skimmed milk lowers the fat content of the sauce. As this sticks rather readily, especially when used in conjunction with low fat spread, keep the heat low and stir continually, use a 'non-stick' saucepan or make the sauce in a bowl in the microwave cooker.

In some recipes you can use some vegetable, or other stock, instead of all milk. This enhances the taste of the sauce and lowers the calorie content.

WHITE SAUCE

25 g/1 oz butter or margarine
25 g/1 oz plain flour or 15 g/½ oz cornflour
300 ml/½ pint milk
salt and pepper

Heat the butter or margarine; stir in the flour or cornflour and continue stirring for 2 or 3 minutes. Add the milk and either stir as the sauce comes to the boil and thickens or allow the milk to come to the boil and whisk very briskly. Season to taste.

This is a sauce with a coating consistency, i.e. it just coats the back of a spoon.

VARIATIONS:
White Sauce – All-in-One Method: Ingredients as above but low fat spread could be used. Put all the ingredients into the saucepan. Place over the heat then stir or whisk as the liquid comes to the boil and the sauce thickens.

MICROWAVE: Use the All-in-One Method and **Full Power**. Remove the bowl from the microwave cooker at regular intervals and whisk briskly to ensure a smooth sauce.

Flavourings for white sauce
Chopped herbs can be added, the most popular being chopped parsley; allow about 2 tablespoons. Add to the thickened sauce.
Cheese Sauce: Add 50 to 75 g/2 to 3 oz cheese to the thickened sauce. Low fat cheeses can be used but see Cheese sauce based on natural yogurt or fromage frais, below.
Mustard Sauce: Add 1 to 2 teaspoons dry English mustard powder to the flour or cornflour or 1 or 2 teaspoons made mustard to the thickened sauce.

LESS USUAL SAUCES

Add chopped parsley or other herbs to natural yogurt or fromage frais.
Cheese Sauce: Add cottage cheese or grated cheese to the yogurt or fromage frais. If heating, put into a basin, stand over hot water.
Speedy Tomato Sauce: Liquidize canned or fresh tomatoes. Heat the purée for a few minutes only with a little garlic salt or garlic juice, seasoning and a dash of soy or Worcestershire sauce.

If you have cooked root vegetables left, sieve, mash or liquidize these until smooth and heat with finely chopped parsley and plenty of seasoning.

DESSERTS

Quite frequently we are told that puddings and desserts are not really good for us. Really, that is a far too sweeping statement. It is true that if we regularly eat rich creamy desserts or puddings that contain a high percentage of fat and sugar there is every possibility we will put on excess weight. The dishes would certainly be ill chosen for anyone following a low cholesterol routine. If, however, the puddings are selected sensibly the ingredients will balance those served at the rest of the meal. Save the luscious rich desserts for special treats to be eaten very occasionally.

Undoubtedly one of the most healthy ways to end a meal is to have fresh fruit. Few desserts are more delicious than a really good fruit salad or fruit compôte with an interesting mixture of flavours. Include some naturally sweet fruits so extra sugar is used sparingly.

You will find traditional puddings on pages 78 and 79 with recipes adjusted to use less fat and sugar.

The interest in low fat alternatives to cream has resulted in the availability of delicious foods like fromage frais, as well as low fat yogurts of all kinds. Fromage frais is a form of fermented milk which is virtually fat free. It makes an excellent accompaniment to hot or cold desserts and is used as an ingredient in both sweet and savoury dishes in this book.

There are many more desserts in this book, providing appetising and nutritious endings to meals.

Fresh fruit desserts
On page 83 are ways to use leftover fruit. Use the recipe for cooking bananas, right, with halved peaches and dessert pears.

BAKED APPLES

2 good-sized cooking apples
little mixed dried fruit, or see method

Core the apples and slit the skins round the middle, even when using a microwave. Fill the centres with mixed dried fruit or diced uncooked dried apricots or prunes or mashed soft fruit. Bake for about 50 minutes in a preheated moderate oven (180°C, 350°F, Gas Mark 4). The natural sugar in dried fruit should be sweetness enough.

MICROWAVE: 4 minutes on **Full Power**.

BANANAS IN LEMON SAUCE

15 g/½ oz margarine
1 tablespoon brown sugar
2 tablespoons lemon juice
4 tablespoons water
3 or 4 small bananas, halved

Heat the margarine in a saucepan, add the sugar, lemon juice and water. Heat over a low heat until the sugar has melted. Add the bananas, cook gently for 3 minutes.

VARIATION:
Make the sauce with the ingredients above. Add 2 tablespoons sultanas or seedless raisins. Heat for 1 minute in the sauce then add the bananas.

MICROWAVE: Use only 3 tablespoons water. Heat the sauce ingredients then add the bananas and cook for 2 minutes on Full Power.

Baked apple (top) and Bananas in lemon sauce, with sultanas (recipes this page)

FRUIT CRUMBLES

You will find various fruit pies on pages 122, 124 and 136, together with different ways of making pastry.

A crumble mixture, however, is easier to make than pastry and it has the advantage that you can use a low fat spread if you wish. Never try to use any product marked 'Very low fat spread' except to spread on bread or toast.

You can make up quite a batch of plain crumble topping, i.e. half fat to flour, and keep it in an airtight container in the refrigerator so it is all ready when needed. Do not keep it more than 2 or 3 weeks.

To make a change, add extra ingredients, such as coconut in the recipe below or the ideas on this page, right.

PEACH AND COCONUT CRUMBLE

For the crumble:
25 g/1 oz butter, margarine or low fat spread
50 g/2 oz flour, preferably plain
25 g/1 oz desiccated coconut
25–40 g/1–1½ oz granulated or soft light brown sugar
1 × 225 g/8 oz can peach slices in syrup or natural juice.
For the sauce:
1 teaspoon arrowroot or cornflour
peach syrup and water (see method)
½–1 tablespoon lemon juice, or to taste
sugar (see method)

Preheat the oven to moderate (180°C,350°F, Gas Mark 4). Rub the selected fat into the flour, add the coconut and sugar.

Drain the peaches; put the syrup on one side for the sauce. Put the peaches into a 600 ml/1 pint pie dish, top with the crumble and bake for 25 minutes.

To make the sauce: blend the arrowroot or cornflour with the peach syrup and lemon juice. You should have 150 ml/¼ pint liquid. Stir over a low heat until thickened. You may add a little sugar.

More crumbles

Use any fresh fruit under the crumble mixture. Cook hard fruit like sliced apples and plums with the minimum of liquid and sugar until nearly soft. Ripe and soft fruit do not require pre-cooking.

Add interest to the crumble topping by the addition of a few chopped nuts or a teaspoon of mixed spice or use wholemeal flour or half flour and half rolled oats.

STEAMED PUDDINGS

The following recipe gives a really light pudding. The ingredients can be mixed by hand with a wooden spoon or you could use an electric mixer or food processor. Make sure the water boils briskly under any light steamed pudding for the first half of the cooking time. This ensures the pudding rises well. After this the water can simmer.

SPONGE PUDDING

75 g/3 oz margarine, preferably polyunsaturated
75 g/3 oz sugar, preferably caster
1 egg
100 g/4 oz self-raising flour or plain flour sifted with 1 teaspoon baking powder
2 tablespoons milk, preferably skimmed
2–3 tablespoons jam or golden syrup

Cream the margarine and sugar until soft and light. Add the egg; beat well. Fold in the flour, or flour and baking powder and milk, or see All-in-One-Method, page 125.

Grease a 900 ml/1½ pint basin. Add the jam or golden syrup. Spoon the sponge mixture over. Cover the basin with greased greaseproof paper and foil. Put into the steamer and cover. Place securely over the saucepan of boiling water and cook for 1¼ hours. Turn out carefully.
Serves 2–4

VARIATIONS:
Use wholemeal flour for extra fibre, plus an extra ½ tablespoon milk.
Reduce both fat and sugar to 50 g/2 oz each; increase the milk to 3 tablespoons.
Use 75 g/3 oz self-raising flour plus ¼ teaspoon baking powder or plain flour with 1 teaspoon baking powder. Add 25 g/1 oz rolled oats for extra flavour and fibre.
Add 1 teaspoon grated lemon or orange rind and use the fruit juice instead of milk.
Add 50–75 g/2–3 oz dried fruit.

MICROWAVE: Cover the basin with clingfilm or absorbent kitchen paper. Allow 6 minutes on **Roast** setting (approximately 66% output – but check manufacturer's book). Stand for 2 minutes. Do not put jam or golden syrup into the basin as in some cookers it burns.
NUTRITIONAL VALUE: A well-balanced pudding especially if smaller amounts of fat and sugar are used. Wholemeal flour and oats add fibre.

MILK PUDDINGS

Most people's ideal milk pudding is one that is very creamy and sweet. This is fine if you are not worried about putting on weight or have not been advised to use skimmed or semi-skimmed milk, instead of full cream, with which you used to make rice and other milk puddings.

The answer is that you should try and make the new kind of pudding quite different, as the suggestions below, so one does not continually 'hark back' and compare it. You will soon agree that the new version has just as much to recommend it as the old type. The first recipe is for the usual rice pudding, the only difference being in the choice of milk. You can adjust other milk puddings in the same way.

RICE PUDDING

40–50 g/1½–2 oz short-grain rice
1 tablespoon sugar, or to taste
600 ml/1 pint milk, full cream, skimmed or
  semi-skimmed

Put the rice, sugar and milk into a 1.2 litre/2 pint pie dish and cook for 2 hours in a slow oven (140–150°C, 275–300° F, Gas Mark 1–2). Stir once or twice if possible; this makes a great deal of difference for it blends the starch with the liquid and the pudding thickens better.
Serves 2–4.

VARIATIONS:
Cook in the top of a double saucepan over boiling water (or use a basin covered with a saucepan lid if you have no double saucepan). This saves fuel and is ideal with skimmed milk, which burns easily, unless using a 'non-stick' saucepan.
Make the pudding more exciting. Put in several tablespoons dried fruit or sliced dried apricots and a little grated lemon rind.
Add diced apple to the rice with sultanas.

MICROWAVE: An ordinary microwave does not make a good rice pudding but a combination cooker is excellent.
NUTRITIONAL VALUE: Rice is an excellent food so enjoy puddings made with this.

FRUIT MOUSSE

1 × 170 g/6 oz can evaporated milk
1 packet fruit-flavoured jelly
water (see method)

Chill the evaporated milk overnight if possible as this makes it so much easier to whip. Open the can just before whipping.

The next day dissolve the jelly in enough boiling water to make up to 450 ml/¾ pint; allow to cool and stiffen to the consistency of a thick syrup. Whip the evaporated milk in another basin then add to the lightly set jelly. Whisk the mixture until light and fluffy. Spoon into glasses.
Serves 4.

NUTRITIONAL VALUE: Evaporated milk is fairly high in fat content. To reduce this, buy light lower fat evaporated milk (generally sold in cartons not cans). For Fresh Fruit Jelly, see page 83.

FRESH FRUIT MOUSSE

1 × 170 g/6 oz can evaporated milk
15 g/½ oz gelatine
450 ml/¾ pint apple, orange, grapefruit or
*   pineapple juice*
sugar (see method)

Chill the evaporated milk, as described in the recipe above. Soften the gelatine in 4 tablespoons of the cold fruit juice then dissolve over a pan of very hot water or in the microwave cooker. If using un-sweetened fruit juice, add a little sugar to taste to this hot mixture.

When the gelatine has dissolved blend with the cold fruit juice. Allow the mixture to set lightly. Whisk the evaporated milk. Continue as the recipe above.
Serves 4

VARIATION:
Use 600 ml/1 pint of thick fruit purée made from cooked fruit or ripe uncooked fruit.

NUTRITIONAL VALUE: Do not heat more than the 4 tablespoons fruit juice or purée to dissolve the gelatine. You retain more of the vitamin value of the fruit if the rest is cold. You also shorten the setting time.

BLACKBERRY AND APPLE CREAMS

225 g/8 oz cooking apples, weight when
*   peeled, cored and sliced*
225 g/8 oz blackberries
150 ml/¼ pint water
40 g/1½ oz granulated sugar
½ tablespoon gelatine
150 ml/¼ pint whipping cream or
*   evaporated milk (see left)*

Cook the apples and blackberries in a saucepan or a bowl in the microwave cooker with half the water and all the sugar until just softened to a purée.

Meanwhile, soften the gelatine by sprinkling it on to the remaining cold water. Stir into the very hot purée and continue stirring until dissolved.

Sieve, liquidize or mash the purée and allow it to cool until it just begins to hold a shape. Whip the cream or evaporated milk then fold into the jelly. Spoon into dishes and allow to set.

VARIATIONS:
Vary the fruit throughout the year.
To make a smoother mixture and one with less fat, substitute low fat natural yogurt or fromage frais for the cream.

Lemon-flavoured Fruit jelly (recipe page 83) and Blackberry and apple creams (recipe this page)

BASED ON YOGURT

One of the easiest and most nutritious of cold desserts is yogurt. Over the years this has become increasingly popular with people of all ages. It is low in Kcalories, especially the low fat type. Plain yogurt is capable of infinite variety. Also, there is an incredible range of flavoured yogurts. In some of these fruit flavouring is used; in others you will find fresh fruit is included.

If you buy natural yogurt you can, of course, add just what fruits you like or use yogurt as a sauce over fruit.

If you become a real 'yogurt lover' then why not make your own? As you will see from the information that follows this is not difficult. It takes time, but during the waiting period you do not have to attend to it – just leave it to its own devices.

To add interest to yogurt
Flavour natural yogurt with grated or ground nutmeg or other spices.

Raisin and Walnut Yogurt: Soak a few seedless raisins in a little sherry or orange juice to soften. Blend with natural yogurt and chopped walnuts.

Crunchy Yogurt: First toast rolled oats. Spread these on a flat metal baking tray, to give a thin layer. Toast for a few minutes under a preheated grill, turning over once or twice, or in a moderate oven (180°C, 350°F, Gas Mark 4) for about 15 minutes. Cool and blend about 15 g/½ oz to each 150 ml/¼ pint natural yogurt. Top the portions with a layer of the oats, a little Demerara sugar and chopped nuts.

Yogurt Cranachan: Blend a tablespoon of toasted oats (as above) with each portion of natural yogurt. Add 1 to 2 teaspoons whisky and top with fresh or defrosted frozen raspberries or other fruit.

TO MAKE YOGURT

While it is possible to buy special electric yogurt makers, consider carefully before buying one. Do you eat sufficient yogurt to justify the expense? It is very possible to make yogurt, without a machine, by the method given below. Undoubtedly, it is cheaper to make yogurt at home than to buy it ready-made.

To start the process you need either a culture (obtainable from a health food store) or a little natural yogurt. A culture is more expensive than the cost of buying natural yogurt.

You need 600 ml/1 pint of milk. If you are anxious to avoid extra fat, use skimmed milk; this produces an acceptable, but rather thin yogurt. For a richer yogurt use full cream milk.

Bring the milk to boiling point in a saucepan on the cooker or in a bowl in the microwave cooker and maintain it at boiling point for 1 to 2 minutes. Do not boil for any longer. Stir well as the milk begins to cool to prevent a skin forming. Allow to cool to 43°C/110°F – or until you can keep your finger in the milk for at least 10 seconds without any discomfort. At this stage, stir at least 3 tablespoons of natural yogurt into the milk.

It is important to keep the milk at 43°C/110°F for 5 to 6 hours. This is the purpose of the electric yogurt maker. The simple alternative is to sterilise a wide-necked vacuum flask with boiled water and to heat the inside of the flask with hot water immediately before using it. Pour away the water and pour the milk into the flask. Put on the cork and cover.

If you have no vacuum flask prepare the yogurt in an ovenproof bowl. Cover the top with clingfilm. Either wrap the bowl in thick cloth and keep in the airing cupboard or cover the bowl with foil and keep in a gas oven that has a pilot light.

Do not move the flask or bowl for the 5 to 6 hours or until it is set. When this stage is reached transfer to a suitable-sized container and place in the refrigerator.

Remember to keep back several tablespoons of the yogurt each time in order to make the next batch.

If you buy long-life milk do not boil this; simply heat it to 43°C/110°F then continue as the methods above.

BASED ON FRUIT

Making a Fresh Fruit Jelly: If you, or a member of the family, do not eat much citrus fruit the answer is to make a fresh fruit jelly. While the whole fruit is better, for it provides fibre as well as vitamin C, the fruit juice still has the vitamin. Do not heat all the juice, for heating will destroy vitamins.

Use 568-scant 600 ml/1 pint juice. Pour 4 tablespoons of this into a basin; sprinkle 15 g/½ oz (1 tablespoon – or 1 envelope) of gelatine on this, or use the same amount of agar-agar if making this for a vegetarian. Allow gelatine to stand for 2 minutes; agar-agar for 10 minutes. Dissolve over a pan of hot water or in the microwave cooker. Stir well then add to the remaining cold juice. Allow to set.
Serves 2–4

Fruit Ambers: To 300 ml/½ pint thick slightly sweetened fruit purée allow 25 g/ 1 oz fine bread or biscuit crumbs and 1 egg yolk. Mix together and spoon into a small pie dish. Bake for 20 minutes at 160°C, 325°F, Gas Mark 3.

Whisk the egg white, fold in 25 g/1 oz caster or light brown sugar. Spoon over the base and continue cooking for another 15 minutes. Serve this fruit dessert hot.

Fruit Fools (foules): Blend equal amounts of thick sweetened custard and thick fruit purée. The fruit need not be absolutely smooth, for the word 'foule' means chopped. If you have no custard then use thick natural yogurt or cottage cheese. Baked apples, skinned and mashed are ideal for this, they are really stiff.

Fruit Pancakes: Make pancakes as the recipe on page 92. Fill with the hot or cold fruit. There is a recipe for Russian Blinis on page 99.

Fruit Sauces: Mash the fruit, sweeten if desired. A fruit sauce can be served with various meats, e.g. apple or plum sauce with pork or duck or as a sweet with ice cream or natural or fruit-flavoured yogurt or cottage cheese.

PEASANT GIRL IN A VEIL

300 ml/½ pint thick lightly sweetened fruit purée, use seasonal fruit such as rhubarb, apples, plums etc
25 g/1 oz butter or margarine
50 g/2 oz soft breadcrumbs
25 g/1 oz Demerara sugar
2–4 tablespoons cream or natural yogurt
25 g/1 oz chocolate, coarsely grated

Allow the fruit purée to become quite cold. Heat the butter or margarine, add the crumbs and cook gently until crisp and brown. Cool then add the sugar.

Arrange layers of the fruit and crumb mixture in dishes, top with the cream or yogurt and the chocolate.

COOKING FOR SUPPER

In this section you will find the lighter dishes that are ideal for supper or for lunch-time, if you prefer to have your main meal in the evening.

In many recipes you will find brief suggestions for preparations that can be made ahead. This is an advantage when thinking about evening meals. You may find you get rather tired by the end of the day, so there is the possibility that you might not bother to prepare a good supper. If the dishes are virtually ready to serve, catering for an evening meal will not be a problem.

Most of the dishes in this section are suitable for a meal on a tray, so you can enjoy not-to-be-missed television programmes. Make supper-time a pleasantly relaxed occasion. Do ensure the tray is well balanced so there is no fear of an accident. What shall we have for supper? There are many foods and dishes that are easily prepared so would be suitable for this meal. It is important to eat sensibly in the evening. If you miss supper, or eat inadequately, you could have a disturbed night because you are hungry. As we get older we feel the cold more; obviously a warm home and warm clothes are important and so is good warming food. All these things help to prevent hypothermia (the term used to denote sub-normal body temperature).

In really cold weather it is a good idea to fill a vacuum flask with a hot drink. If you feel chilly in the night this will be at hand to warm you.

The recipes in this section range from a variety of cooked dishes to the simple toasted snacks and sandwiches given on page 86. These can be prepared earlier in the day. They keep fresh if wrapped and stored in the refrigerator. Soup makes a splendid dish for supper. There are recipes on pages 26–34.

Toasted snacks (recipes page 86) – from the top, roes, sardines, cheese and mushrooms

INTERESTING SANDWICHES

Sandwiches for supper can have a fairly generous amount of filling. Use wholemeal bread, to provide extra fibre, or one of the white breads with fibre added. For a change, try pitta bread.

Based on cheese
Blend cottage or curd cheese with finely chopped dates or seedless raisins or chopped pineapple or grated apple. Mix equal quantities of grated cheese and grated raw carrot with mayonnaise or natural yogurt to bind. For a hearty sandwich, mash cooked or canned beans and blend with cheese.

Based on eggs
Hard-boil the eggs, chop and mix with a little mayonnaise, finely diced red or green pepper or chopped watercress or skinned chopped tomatoes. Put fingers of Tortilla (see page 88), between buttered rolls or slices of bread or on crispbread.

Based on fish
Blend one of the fish pâtés (see pages 24) with finely chopped cucumber. Blend peeled prawns with a little mayonnaise and chopped cucumber or tomato. Blend flaked cooked kipper or smoked mackerel or mashed sardines with watercress.

Based on meats
Sliced ham, tongue, chicken and other cold meats including salami make good sandwich fillings but can be a little dry, so chop the meat and blend with cottage cheese or with thick chutney or chopped mustard pickle (if this blends with the meat) and thinly sliced raw button mushrooms.

TOASTED SNACKS

The following make good supper dishes. Spread the hot toast with yeast extract for extra vitamins instead of, or in addition to, the butter or margarine or low fat spread.

Mushrooms on toast
Cook mushrooms in a little hot butter or margarine or oil in a saucepan or frying pan for 3 to 4 minutes or for approximately 2 minutes on Full Power in the microwave cooker. If you are anxious to avoid using fat then cook the mushrooms for the same time in seasoned water. Strain well before putting on the hot toast. A crushed garlic clove and a little chopped parsley add flavour.

Roes on toast
Poach soft herring roes in a little seasoned milk or white wine for about 6 minutes or until they turn opaque (milky), or steam over boiling water for the same time. Drain and serve on toast. Hard roes should be coated in a very little flour and fried.

Sardines on toast
Drain sardines canned in oil; place the whole or mashed sardines on the hot toast. Do not remove bones, for these contain valuable calcium.

Toasted cheese
Use grated or sliced cheese or the Cheese spread on page 91. Spread over the hot toast and put under the pre-heated grill until the cheese begins to bubble.

If you prefer to melt the cheese very quickly, put the toast, covered with the cheese, into the microwave and leave on Full Power for 20 to 30 seconds.

EGG DISHES

All the favourite ways of serving eggs, i.e. boiled, fried, poached and scrambled are very suitable for supper dishes providing they are cooked as advocated by health authorities. Omelettes must be cooked until firm, and not soft and slightly runny.

When this book was written there was a considerable problem regarding the spread of salmonella enteritidis, the most vulnerable being the very young, the elderly, those who are unwell and pregnant women.

It is advocated that eggs are cooked until firm so they reach a sufficiently high temperature to ensure the risk of salmonella is no longer present. Avoid uncooked eggs.

You may have been advised to limit your intake of eggs, due to their cholesterol content; page 128 gives more details.

EGG SALADS

Hard-boiled eggs can form the basis of interesting salads. Put the eggs into boiling water and cook for 8–10 minutes. Crack the shells and put the cooked eggs into cold water to prevent the formation of a dark line around the yolks. Shell the eggs and serve with mixed salad ingredients and a cooked-egg mayonnaise (see right).

The eggs can be given extra flavour, as in the following suggestions.
Anchovy Eggs: Remove the yolks into a basin, mash and mix with a little mayonnaise and enough anchovy sauce or anchovy spread to flavour. Spoon the mixture back into the whites.

Small amounts of various pâtés can be used in the same way.
Curried Eggs: Remove the yolks into a basin, mash and mix with a little mayonnaise or smooth chutney and curry powder or curry paste to taste. Spoon the mixture back into the egg whites.

NOTE: Mayonnaise can be made without raw eggs. For Hard-boiled Egg Mayonnaise: Rub the yolks of 2 hard-boiled eggs through a sieve or mash finely. Blend with a little salt and pepper, 1 teaspoon French or made English mustard and a pinch of sugar. Gradually beat in *up to* 150 ml/¼ pint oil; add a little lemon juice or white wine vinegar.
Tofu Dressing: Beat or liquidize 297 g/10½ oz (average packet) thin (silken) tofu with 2–3 tablespoons oil, 2 tablespoons lemon juice or white wine vinegar, seasoning and a little sugar or honey to taste.

SAVOURY EGGS

For the sauce:
½ tablespoon corn oil
2 medium tomatoes, skinned and chopped
1 tablespoon tomato purée
1 tablespoon chopped parsley
4 tablespoons fromage frais
salt and pepper
1 teaspoon lemon juice

2–4 eggs
salad (optional)

Heat the oil, add the tomatoes and cook for 5 minutes then add the other sauce ingredients. Hard-boil, shell and halve the eggs.

To serve hot: Heat the sauce for a few minutes, but do not allow to boil. Spoon over the eggs and serve with hot toast or rolls.

To serve cold: Chill the sauce. Arrange the eggs on a bed of salad.

VARIATION:
Add 1 crushed garlic clove to the sauce.

HAM SOUFFLÉ OMELETTE

3–4 eggs, separated
50 g/2 oz cooked ham, finely chopped
1–2 tablespoons chopped chives or spring
* onions*
salt and pepper
½ tablespoon plain flour
1 tablespoon milk
25 g/1 oz butter
25 g/1 oz mushrooms, thinly sliced

Blend the egg yolks with the ham, chives or spring onions, a little seasoning, the flour and milk. Whisk the egg whites until very stiff in another basin. Fold the egg whites into the egg yolk mixture. Cover the basin.

Heat the butter in an omelette or frying pan at least 18 cm/7 inch in diameter. Add the mushrooms and cook for 3 minutes. Meanwhile, pre-heat the grill. Pour the egg mixture over the mushrooms and cook steadily for 2 minutes. Place the omelette pan under the heated grill, making certain the handle is well away from the heat. Cook until the omelette is set on top.

Make a slit across the centre of the omelette. Fold away from the handle and tip on to a hot dish.

VARIATIONS:
Haddock Soufflé Omelette: Substitute 75 g/3 oz flaked cooked fresh or smoked haddock for the ham.
Cheese Soufflé Omelette: Substitute 50 g/2 oz grated cheese or cottage cheese for the cooked ham.

NUTRITIONAL VALUE: A high protein supper dish. Fairly high in fat.

Preparing for supper: Chop or flake flavouring. Keep them well covered in the refrigerator.

SWEDISH BAKED OMELETTE

For the vegetable mixture:
25 g/1 oz butter or margarine or 1
* tablespoon oil*
few cooked carrots, or other cooked
* vegetable, neatly diced*
1 large tomato, skinned and chopped
50 g/2 oz mushrooms, sliced

3 or 4 eggs
2 tablespoons water
salt and pepper
1 tablespoon chopped parsley

Preheat the oven to moderately hot (200°C, 400°F, Gas Mark 6).

Put the butter, margarine or oil with the vegetables in a small ovenproof dish, cover with a piece of foil or a lid. Heat for 5 to 6 minutes. Beat the eggs with the water, a little seasoning and the parsley.

Pour over the hot vegetables and bake for 15 minutes for firmly set eggs.

VARIATION:
Tortilla: This can be made with virtually the same ingredients as above although the traditional recipe is often based on potatoes and onions. Cook the vegetables in the butter, margarine or oil in an omelette pan. Beat the eggs with the water and a little seasoning. Pour over the hot vegetables and cook steadily until firm.

MICROWAVE: Halve the amount of fat; put into a dish with the vegetables, cover. Cook for 2 minutes on **Full Power**. Add the beaten eggs mixture and cook for 3 or 4 minutes.

Ham soufflé omelette (top) and Swedish baked omelette (recipes this page)

CHEESE DISHES

Cheese is a good choice for light supper dishes although a few people find it slightly indigestible if they eat it in the evening just before going to bed. Cheese is high in protein and in calcium.

Most cheese has a fairly high fat and Kcalorie content; exceptions are cottage cheese and the special low fat cheeses now available. This means that if you are trying to lose weight, or have to restrict the fat intake in your diet, just limit the amount of cheese you eat or choose the variety carefully. Be aware, too, of current health authority guidelines on soft cheeses.

Cheese is the basis of a wide range of dishes that would be enjoyable at suppertime. Nothing is more simple than cheese with biscuits or bread. Add a simple salad and you have a good meal. Toasted cheese or cheese sandwiches take little effort to prepare.

If you enjoy a cheese sauce over mixed vegetables or cauliflower or hard-boiled eggs, you can prepare this dish earlier in the day. Top the food with a good layer of crisp breadcrumbs and heat in the oven or microwave cooker. While a cheese pudding or cheese soufflé needs cooking at the last minute, some of the preparations can be made ahead (see below and page 95).

CHEESE SOUFFLÉ

15 g/1/2 oz plain flour
50–75 g/2–3 oz Cheddar or Gruyère or other cheese, finely grated
5 tablespoons milk
salt and pepper
1/2–1 teaspoon made mustard
2 eggs
1 egg white (optional)

Preheat the oven to moderate (180°C, 350°F, Gas Mark 4). Grease a 12.5 cm/5 inch soufflé dish.

Put the flour and cheese into a basin and mix together. The amount of cheese used depends on personal taste and the strength of flavour of the particular cheese. Bring the milk to the boil, pour approximately half over the flour and cheese, stirring all the time, then add the rest of the milk. Return the ingredients to the saucepan and cook over a moderate heat for 1 minute, or until the mixture binds. Remove from the heat and add the seasonings.

Separate the eggs and beat the yolks into the cheese mixture. Whisk the 2 or 3 egg whites until they just stand in soft peaks. Beat a little into the cheese mixture to give a softer texture then fold the remainder of the egg whites into the other ingredients. Spoon into the soufflé dish and bake for approximately 20 to 25 minutes or until well risen and golden brown. Serve at once.

VARIATIONS:

This is an excellent dish in which to use leftover cheese. The low fat cheeses can also be used. Do not be afraid of mixing the kinds of cheese. Blue cheeses cook well and Brie or Camembert are delicious. Cottage cheese and fromage frais are not suitable.

MICROWAVE: Use this to heat the milk and to cook the flour and cheese for approximately 30 seconds on **Full Power**.
NUTRITIONAL VALUE: The dish is high in protein and calcium. The amount of fat will vary according to the cheese used.

NOTE: If you use a 15–18 cm/6–7 inch soufflé dish cook at 190°C, 375°F, Gas Mark 5 for a few minutes shorter time.

Preparing for supper: Blend the grated cheese and flour in a bowl.

CHEESE SPREAD

This is an ideal way of using up oddments of cheese. While it can be prepared with one kind of cheese it is more interesting if you combine two or more varieties. A blue cheese is excellent with a curd cheese or you could try a milder Cheddar, Edam or Gouda cheese.

Store in the refrigerator or, if you feel you may not use it all within 2 weeks, put into small containers in the freezer. It is a good idea to pack just enough for one meal in each container.

Use the spread on hot toast or as a sandwich filling. The amount in the recipe would be sufficient for about 6 large slices of hot toast or a filling for 8 good-sized sandwiches.

225 g/8 oz cheese, grated or crumbled
50 g/2 oz butter or margarine, slightly softened
1 tablespoon dry sherry
few drops Worcestershire sauce
½–1 teaspoon French mustard or made English mustard
freshly ground black pepper

Blend all the ingredients together until smooth. The cheese could be put into a food processor without grating. Switch on for a few seconds then add the remaining ingredients and process again for a few seconds.

Spread the mixture evenly on hot toast and heat under the grill to melt.

FREEZING: This freezes well.
NUTRITIONAL VALUE: Cheese is an excellent source of calcium and protein. Many cheeses are high in fat. If you wish to lower the fat content choose Edam cheese or one of the low fat varieties.

CHEESE PUDDING

150 ml/¼ pint milk
15 g/½ oz butter or margarine
50 g/2 oz soft wholemeal or white breadcrumbs
50–75 g/2–3 oz Cheddar or other cheese, grated
1 large egg
salt and pepper

Heat the milk with the butter or margarine until this melts. Remove from the heat and add the breadcrumbs. Allow to stand for at least 15 minutes. Stir in the cheese, beaten egg and a little salt and pepper.

Spoon into a lightly greased 600 ml/1 pint pie dish and bake in the centre of a preheated moderately hot oven (200°C, 400°F, Gas Mark 6) for 20 minutes or until well risen. Serve as soon as cooked.

VARIATIONS:
For a lighter pudding use 225 ml/7½ fl oz milk and 2 eggs. Bake for 25 minutes.
Ham and Cheese Pudding: Use only 25 g/1 oz cheese and 50 g/2 oz diced cooked ham.

NUTRITIONAL VALUE: An easy and well balanced supper dish. To reduce fat, choose skimmed milk and low fat cheese.

CHEESE-FILLED POTATOES

Bake good-sized potatoes. When cooked, cut a slice from each potato and scoop out most of the potato pulp. Mash this with cottage cheese, then add a little seasoning plus a generous amount of chopped parsley or chives. Spoon the mixture back into the potato skins. Top with grated cheese and heat for a short time.

MAKING PANCAKES

Pancakes are incredibly versatile since they can be filled with sweet or savoury ingredients. Try making the batter with wholemeal or brown flour, which has a very good flavour; or use equal quantities of white and wholemeal flour.

100 g/4 oz plain white or wholemeal flour
pinch salt
1 egg
275 ml*/½ pint milk or milk and water
little oil for frying
*use this metrication

Blend the ingredients and beat until smooth. Heat just a few drops of oil in the pan; pour in enough batter to give a thin coating. Cook for 1½ to 2 minutes. You can tell when the pancake is cooked on the first side as it moves easily in the pan. Turn the pancake and cook on the second side.

Continue until all the batter is used to make 12 to 16 small pancakes. After cooking the first pancake you should need little, if any, extra oil if your pan is reasonably 'good-tempered'. No oil is needed with a 'non-stick' pan.

To keep the pancakes hot, separate them with squares of greased greaseproof paper and put on a heat-resistant dish over a pan of boiling water or in a cool oven.

FREEZING: Add 1 tablespoon oil or melted butter or margarine to the batter just before cooking the pancakes, to improve the texture. Separate as above, before wrapping, so you can 'peel off' the required number.
Put a little sauce *under* as well as over filled pancakes if they are to be reheated.

VEGETABLE PANCAKES

For the savoury tomato sauce:
1 small onion, finely chopped or grated
4 medium tomatoes, skinned and chopped
150 ml/¼ pint water
few basil leaves or pinch dried basil
  (optional)
salt and pepper
For the filling:
175 g/6 oz mixed cooked vegetables, e.g.
  diced carrots, beans and peas or to taste

4 pancakes (see recipe, left)

Put the ingredients for the sauce into a pan. Cover tightly and simmer for 15 to 20 minutes. Remove the basil leaves. For a smoother sauce, blend the ingredients in a liquidizer. Mix the cooked vegetables with about 2 tablespoons of the tomato sauce. Fill the pancakes with the vegetable mixture, roll firmly and put into an ovenproof dish. Top with the sauce and heat for about 15 minutes in a preheated oven (180°C, 350°F, Gas Mark 4).

VARIATIONS:
Use White or Cheese sauce (see page 75) instead of tomato sauce.

FREEZING: These filled pancakes freeze well; follow tips for freezing pancakes (left).
MICROWAVE: Heat the filled and coated pancakes for 5 minutes on **Full Power**.
NUTRITIONAL VALUE: Pancakes are higher in fibre, if wholemeal flour is used.

Preparing for supper: Pour a little sauce into the dish; add the filled pancakes and sauce. Keep cool until ready to cook.

Pancakes with a green vegetable filling and cheese sauce (recipe this page)

FISH DISHES

Fish is an ideal food for a light evening meal, for it is easy to digest and quick to cook as well.

Canned salmon and tuna can be used as a filling for sandwiches or served with a mixed salad. Sardines or roes are excellent on toast (see page 86). Smoked haddock can be served poached or made into a simple kedgeree. The simplest way of cooking the haddock is to buy the frozen 'boil in the bag' product and just place this in a pan of water and cook as the instructions given. If you have a good fishmonger buy a small whole haddock or piece of haddock fillet. Cut this into portions and cook for 5 to 7 minutes in gently simmering water. It is worthwhile cooking extra to make the Kedgeree on this page.

KEDGEREE

25 g/1 oz butter or margarine
3 tablespoons milk
175 g/6 oz cooked smoked haddock, flaked
175 g/6 oz cooked long-grain rice

Heat the butter or margarine and the milk; add the fish and rice. Heat gently.

VARIATIONS:
Add a chopped hard-boiled egg and a little chopped parsley to the rice mixture when nearly ready to serve.
Kedgeree Salad: Omit the butter or margarine, blend the cooked fish and cooked rice with 2 tablespoons mayonnaise; allow to cool. Add 2 tablespoons chopped spring onions, 2 or 3 tablespoons peeled and chopped cucumber and any other salad vegetables you have available. Serve with sliced tomatoes.

FREEZING: It is a good idea to cook a fairly large batch of rice then divide this into portions and freeze these. Defrost and use as required.

NOTE: To give 175 g/6 oz cooked rice you need 50 g/2 oz uncooked rice.

Preparing for supper: Have all the ingredients ready for the hot Kedgeree. Heat for a few minutes.

FISH CAKES

175 g/6 oz cooked white fish or salmon or
    canned salmon or tuna
175 g/6 oz mashed potatoes
2 teaspoons chopped parsley (optional)
1 egg, beaten
salt and pepper
2 teaspoons plain flour
25 g/1 oz crisp breadcrumbs
oil (see method)

Flake the fish very finely; if using canned fish drain this well. Blend the fish, potatoes, parsley, half the egg and a little seasoning.

Form into 4 to 6 round cakes. Dust with the flour, then brush with the rest of the beaten egg and coat in the breadcrumbs.

Either fry the fish cakes for 4 to 5 minutes in the minimum of hot oil in a frying pan, turning them over so they become brown on either side, or cook them in the oven on a preheated greased baking sheet (see page 38 for details).

Serve very hot with baked tomatoes.
Serves 2–3

FREEZING: Open-freeze so the coating is not harmed, then pack. Cook from frozen.

Preparing for supper: Make the Fish cakes when convenient, chill well or freeze. The cakes keep a better shape if they are really cold when put into the frying pan or oven.

MAKING A SOUFFLÉ

Soufflés are really very simple to make. They just consist of a basic purée or sauce, the flavouring and the eggs. The eggs are separated and the whites whisked to incorporate air into the mixture and produce a wonderfully light dish.

It really is better to make soufflés when you are cosily at home, for the only problem about this dish is that it must not be kept waiting. It should be eaten as soon as it comes from the oven. The following recipe is suitable for cooked fish or canned salmon or tuna or shellfish.

FISH SOUFFLÉ

25 g/1 oz butter or margarine
25 g/1 oz plain flour
150 ml/¼ pint milk
2 eggs, separated
100 g/4 oz cooked fish, flaked or finely
* chopped*
salt and pepper
1 egg white

Grease the inside of a 15–18 cm/6–7 inch soufflé dish. Preheat the oven to moderately hot (190°C, 375°F, Gas Mark 5).

Melt the butter or margarine in a good-sized saucepan and stir in the flour. Add the milk and stir or whisk briskly over a low heat until a thick binding sauce (a panada) results. Remove the pan from the heat. Add the egg yolks and the fish to the sauce. Mix thoroughly and add seasoning to taste.

Whisk the egg whites until they stand in soft peaks, beat a tablespoon into the fish mixture to give a softer consistency then fold in the remaining egg whites.

Spoon into the soufflé dish and bake for 25 minutes or until well-risen and golden.

VARIATIONS:
A luxury soufflé for special occasions can be made with chopped smoked salmon.
Cheese Soufflé: Can be made as the recipe above, instead of the method given on page 90; in this case used the sized dish given in the basic recipe and cook at the slightly higher temperature, i.e. 190°C, 375°F, Gas Mark 5 for 20 to 25 minutes.
Chicken Soufflé: Follow the recipe for Fish Soufflé, but use minced or finely chopped cooked chicken instead of fish and 150 ml/¼ pint chicken stock plus 2 tablespoons milk instead of all milk, as in the recipe. The extra amount of liquid gives a softer and moist texture to the mixture.

Tiny pieces of pheasant can be used instead of chicken.
Vegetable Soufflés: Make a 150 ml/¼ pint purée of your favourite vegetables, e.g. cooked asparagus, artichokes, carrots, spinach or use uncooked tomato purée. Use this plus 2 tablespoons milk to make the sauce as the method given in the basic recipe. The other way to prepare a vegetable soufflé is to put a layer of cooked vegetables at the bottom of the dish then top this with a cheese or fish or chicken soufflé mixture. Bake for approximately 35 minutes at 180°C, 350°F, Gas Mark 4 to make sure the bottom layer of vegetables becomes really heated.
NOTE: You can prepare the soufflé completely then put the mixture into the soufflé dish. Cover this with a mixing bowl to exclude all air. The soufflé will stand for up to 1 hour before being cooked.
Preparing for supper: Prepare the ingredients earlier; unfortunately you must do the final mixing later in the day, but see NOTE above.

95

MEAT DISHES

Throughout this book you will find a variety of easy dishes using meat and poultry, some of which are light and therefore ideal for an evening meal.

You could adapt the recipes for Orange chicken and Milanaise chicken on this page, using slices of cooked ham or cooked tongue instead.

The following recipe is ideal for a meal that uses only a very small amount of meat. As you will see from the ingredients that follow, you could use any cooked meat, including the interesting kinds of salami available nowadays.

MEAT RICE SALAD

100 g/4 oz brown or white long-grain rice
salt and pepper
2 tablespoons mayonnaise
50–100 g/2–4 oz button mushrooms, thinly
*   sliced*
few cooked peas
1 or 2 carrots, grated
25–50 g/1–2 oz nuts, see page 155 for
wise
175 g/6 oz cooked meat, neatly diced
natural yogurt to bind

Cook the rice in your favourite way, or as instructed on the packet, adding a little seasoning to the water to give it plenty of flavour. You will find the method of cooking rice in a microwave cooker on page 98.

Strain and blend with the mayonnaise while hot. Allow to cool then blend in the raw mushrooms, peas, carrots, nuts and the meat. Add a little yogurt to make a fairly soft mixture. Serve with a green salad.

NOTE: When serving mushrooms raw, make sure they are small and very fresh.

ORANGE CHICKEN

2 portions chicken, ready cooked (see p. 64)
1 teaspoon cornflour
150 ml/¼ pint orange juice
1 teaspoon soy sauce
salt and pepper
1 tablespoon blanched flaked almonds
To garnish:
watercress
1 small orange, sliced

The portions of chicken can be left whole or the flesh may be cut into neat strips. Blend the cornflour with the orange juice and soy sauce. Pour into a good-sized frying pan and stir over a medium heat until the sauce thickens slightly. Add a little seasoning and the chicken. Heat for 5 minutes if the chicken has been cut into small pieces or about 8–10 minutes if the joints are left whole. Add the almonds and serve garnished with watercress and orange slices.

VARIATION:
Milanaise Chicken: Omit the orange juice and almonds. Use 225 ml/7½ fl oz tomato juice or purée made by liquidizing fresh tomatoes or 2 tablespoons tomato purée from a can or tube, made up to 225 ml/7½ fl oz with water or chicken stock, plus a finely chopped or grated onion. Simmer the onion in the tomato mixture for 5 minutes after this has thickened slightly, then add the chicken plus soy sauce.

Preparing for supper: Make the sauce, cooking until it has thickened. Add the chicken and almonds. Do not heat but pour into a dish and cover. Heat in the oven or microwave just before the meal.

Artichokes (left – recipe on page 98) and Meat rice salad (recipe this page)

LUXURY VEGETABLES

As the delicious young vegetables come into season, it is sensible to enjoy them as a main course, rather than an accompaniment to other foods.

Globe artichokes
Allow 1 large or 2 small artichokes per person. Cut off the stems; pull away any discoloured outer leaves. You may trim the tips of the leaves with kitchen scissors.

Heat 600 ml/1 pint of water; if you have an enamel saucepan use this, for the artichokes keep a better colour. Add a very little salt and 1 to 2 teaspoons lemon juice. Boil the water, add the artichokes. Cover the pan. The cooking time varies, so test after 12 to 15 minutes; the average time for large artichokes is 25 minutes. The vegetable is cooked when you can pull away a leaf and the base is soft; drain and remove the centre (choke) with a spoon.

Serve hot with butter or margarine or with lemon juice, or cold with mayonnaise or an oil and lemon juice dressing or with cottage cheese or fromage frais.

Asparagus
Trim the white ends of the stalks. If you have a very deep pan the stalks can stand upright. You could put them in a basket (type for frying or blanching vegetables for freezing). If you do not have this, tie the asparagus in bundles (one per person) with fine string. The stalks can lie flat in a saucepan or deep frying pan.

Bring the water to the boil, add a little salt and the vegetable. The cooking time for thin stalks can be as little as 10 minutes; thick ones up to 20 to 25 minutes.

VEGETABLE RISOTTO

Heat a tablespoon of oil in a good-sized pan, add 1 or 2 chopped onions, cook for several minutes then stir in 100 g/4 oz medium-grain (risotto) rice or long-grain brown or white rice. Blend well then add 100 g/4 oz sliced mushrooms, 1 or 2 chopped tomatoes, 600 ml/1 pint water and season lightly.

Bring to simmering point and cover the pan. Check after 15 minutes on the tenderness of the rice; if nearly cooked, as medium-grain rice will be, remove the lid so the excess moisture evaporates and cook until a sticky consistency.

MICROWAVE COOKED RICE

The cooking time in a microwave is not substantially different from that used when cooking rice in a saucepan but the bowl will not boil dry and is easier to wash up than a pan. Rice varies, so the times below are approximate and if cold water is used, the cooking time is longer.

Allow 550 ml/18 fl oz (just under 1 pint) boiling water to each 100 g/4 oz rice. The cooking times are based on this amount. Put the rice, water, 1 teaspoon oil and salt to taste in a container of at least 2.5 litre/4 pint capacity.

Cover and cook on **Full Power**.

Long-grain white rice – 8 to 10 minutes
Par-boiled white rice – 9 to 11 minutes
Brown or Basmati rice – 18 to 20 minutes
Frozen cooked rice – 2 to 3 minutes, or as packet instructions.

Allow to stand for 5 minutes then test. Strain if necessary.

SUPPER-TIME DESSERTS

Although you may not want a hot or cold dessert every evening and would prefer to have fresh fruit, there will be occasions when you have just a light savoury course and feel some kind of dessert is necessary to complete the meal.

If you have rice pudding left over you can turn this into an appetising cold dish. The quantities given are approximate since these can be varied, according to taste.

The Russian Blinis could be called a complete light meal, since you have the food value of pancakes, cheese and fruit.

RICE CONDÉ

300 ml/½ pint rice pudding (see page 79)
4 tablespoons whipping cream*
fresh or cooked fruit (see method)
1 tablespoon water
3 tablespoons redcurrant jelly
*contains less fat than double cream

The rice pudding must be quite cold before adding the cream. Whip the cream and blend with the pudding. Spoon the condé into 2 dishes.

Top with the fruit, such as sliced well-drained cooked or canned apricots, sliced peaches or fresh fruit such as orange slices, raspberries or strawberries.

Heat the water and jelly until a spreading consistency. Cool for a minute then spread over the fruit.

VARIATIONS:
Use thick natural yogurt or slightly sweetened cottage cheese instead of the whipping cream.

Empress Rice: Fold the whipped cream or yogurt or sweetened cottage cheese into the cold rice pudding. Add 2 tablespoons seedless raisins or sultanas, 1 tablespoon chopped glacé cherries and 1 tablespoon sweet sherry. Spoon into 2 dishes. Add a topping of apricot jam; this gives additional flavour and keeps the pudding moist.

RUSSIAN BLINIS

4 pancakes (see page 92)
4 tablespoons cottage cheese
4 tablespoons hot or cold fresh fruit purée

If making pancakes just before the meal you can keep the 4 required hot (see page 92). If prepared ahead, see the advice under Preparing for supper (page 84).

Fill the hot pancakes with the uncooked cheese and the fruit purée. Fold or roll and serve at once.

VARIATION:
Surprise Pancakes: Fill hot pancakes with hot fruit purée and spoonfuls of really firm ice cream, fold or roll and serve at once.

NOTE: After making the 4 pancakes, put the rest of the batter into a covered container and keep in the refrigerator until the next day to use for more pancakes or a small Yorkshire pudding. Whisk well before using. Do not store the batter longer than 24 hours.

Preparing for supper: If you have cooked the pancakes earlier, reheat for a few minutes in a covered dish in a moderately hot oven or 1 or 2 minutes in the microwave cooker. If you have taken them from the freezer heat on **Defrost** setting in the microwave for 3 to 4 minutes or 15 minutes in a covered dish in a moderate oven (160°C, 325°F, Gas Mark 3).

EATING OUT-OF-DOORS

Most people would agree that food tastes better eaten out-of-doors; the fresh air certainly stimulates one's appetite. The great asset of being at home with greater freedom is that you can take advantage of a sudden spell of good weather, pack a picnic, and be on your way to a favourite haunt or outdoor function.

Quite a number of the dishes in this chapter freeze well. It is a good idea to prepare them when you have time, so they are ready when needed. You will not be delayed by making preparations.

The kind of picnic food you carry depends very much on your mode of transport. If you are travelling by car it can be quite an ambitious meal. If walking, or using public transport, a neater package will be more suitable.

You certainly will be a 'winner' with the younger generation if you invite them to a barbecue; they always enjoy the informality of eating out-of-doors.

Barbecue food is basically very simple. Treat the recipes on page 107 as the 'blue print' for cooking other kinds of meat and fish. Most men are extremely proficient at barbecue cooking and enjoy an opportunity to prove their skill.

Your picnics need not entail long journeys – you can have delightful picnic meals in the garden. While you could serve the usual food, it makes it more of an occasion if you prepare the kind of dishes you would take on a proper picnic.

If you are entertaining young children, and the weather is fine, then plan an outdoor meal for them. No worry about restless youngsters wanting to get down from the table. Serve the picnic on the lawn and avoid accidents by giving the children easy-to-manage food on disposable plates.

A well-stocked picnic basket can make any day out a special occasion

PACKING A PICNIC

A picnic menu can be based on sandwiches plus a hot or cold beverage. This would probably be an ideal choice if you are walking to your destination, or going by public transport. Bread is an excellent food and the filling should be chosen to add not only an interesting flavour, but extra nourishment as well. The sandwich fillings on page 86 would be just as suitable for a picnic as for an informal supper. Check that the fillings are not too moist; if they are, the bread is inclined to become soggy.

You can, of course, have an even easier meal to prepare. Take fresh rolls plus cheese or hard-boiled eggs and slices of meat, or off a meat loaf, such as the Fruited beef loaf on page 104.

There are many ways of making a pizza; the recipe that starts on this page, for instance, is based on a scone-type base. If you make yeast bread you will probably prefer to use some of that type of dough for the base, as in the recipe on page 103.

Freezing sandwiches

It does take time to cut sandwiches, and that could be a nuisance if the weather is glorious and you are anxious to be on your way. Why not prepare a good batch of sandwiches when you have time and freeze them? Do not freeze any that have salad ingredients in them for this becomes limp and inedible. Cooked eggs are to be avoided as they become tough and 'rubbery'.

If you are travelling a little distance, do not defrost the frozen sandwiches; you will find that by the time you reach your destination they will have thawed out and be in perfect condition.

EASY PIZZA

For the tomato layer:
1 tablespoon oil
1 medium onion, finely chopped or grated
1 or 2 garlic cloves, crushed
450 g/1 lb tomatoes, skinned and chopped
salt and pepper
1 teaspoon finely chopped oregano or ½
    teaspoon dried oregano
For the base:
150 g/5 oz self-raising flour or plain flour
    sifted with 1¼ teaspoons baking powder
25 g/1 oz butter or margarine
milk to mix
For the topping:
50-100 g/2-4 oz cheese (see method)
few anchovy fillets
few black or green olives

Heat the oil, add the onion and garlic and cook for several minutes. Add the tomatoes, cover the saucepan, and simmer gently for about 15 minutes, or until a thick purée. If the mixture is a little thin and 'watery' boil briskly for a minute or so without the lid on the pan. Add seasoning and oregano and allow to cool.

Preheat the oven before preparing the base. If you are making a thin pizza, set to hot (220°C, 425°F, Gas Mark 7). Use a slightly lower setting (200°C, 400°F, Gas Mark 6) if you are making a thicker base.

To make the base: sift the flour, or flour and baking powder, with a generous amount of seasoning; rub in the butter or margarine. Add enough milk to make a soft rolling consistency.

Roll out the dough on a lightly floured board until it is just over 6 mm/¼ inch in thickness if you like a rather thin pizza, or make it up to 1.5 cm/½ inch in thickness if you prefer it to be thicker. Form into a neat round, square or oblong. Place on an ungreased baking sheet.

Spread the thick tomato mixture over the base. Grate or thinly slice the cheese. The ideal type is Mozzarella, but this is expensive, so you may like to use Cheddar, or any other cheese of a good cooking variety which you may have. Spread the cheese over the tomato mixture.

Bake for approximately 7 to 10 minutes, depending on the thickness of the base, then carefully arrange the anchovy fillets and olives over the top of the pizza and return to the oven for a further 10 minutes, or until the base if firm.
Serves 4-5

VARIATIONS:
To give more flavour to the tomato topping, stir 1 tablespoon tomato purée into the other ingredients when these have formed a thick purée.
Bacon Pizza: Partially cook the pizza, as the basic recipe, then add a lattice of lean bacon strips and return to the oven to complete.
Fish Pizza: Omit the anchovy fillets and olives, and place cooked fish or shellfish under the cheese topping; cook as above.
Vegetarian Pizza: Put a layer of cooked beans or other cooked vegetables under the cheese layer and continue cooking as the basic recipe. If you are cooking this for a Vegan, who will not eat cheese, then partially cook the pizza as the basic recipe, top the tomato mixture with a layer of cooked vegetables; cover these with a piece of foil and return to the oven. The vegetables will become hot, and the scone dough continue to cook without the tomato topping becoming dry and unappetising.

FREEZING: These pizzas are too large for one or two portions, so cut into sections when cold and before freezing. Place on a tray and freeze without wrapping, so the tomato topping is not spoiled, then wrap.

CLASSIC PIZZA

For the tomato layer:
ingredients as in the recipe on page 102
For the dough:
Basic bread dough (see page 116); if making specially, use just 225 g/8 oz flour etc; or take about 1/6th from the 'proven' bread dough made with 1.3 kg/3 lb flour few drops oil
For the topping:
ingredients as the basic recipe on page 102 or any of the variations above

Prepare the tomato layer, and allow to cool.

Make the bread and after it has 'proved' (risen), roll out until just about 6 mm/¼ inch thick. Brush the dough with a few drops of oil then cover with the tomato mixture. Cover lightly with oiled clingfilm and allow the dough to 'prove' for approximately 30 minutes. Top with the cheese.

Preheat the oven during the 'proving' time to hot (220°C, 425°F, Gas Mark 7).

Bake the pizza for 10 minutes then remove from the oven and top with the anchovy fillets and olives. Lower the heat to 190°C, 375°F, Gas Mark 5; return the pizza to the oven and continue cooking for 10 to 15 minutes.
Serves 4-5

VARIATION:
Deep-Dish Pizza: The yeast dough is very suitable for this type of pizza. Make twice the amount of the tomato mixture. Roll out the dough until very thin, almost like pastry. Line the base and sides of a 20–23 cm/8–9 inch sandwich tin. Fill with the tomato mixture. Allow to 'prove' and continue as the basic recipe.

NUTRITIONAL VALUE: Excellent dishes, low in fat if not too much cheese is used.

MAKING A MEAT LOAF

The recipe that follows makes one of the nicest meat shapes. It is ideal for a picnic since it keeps beautifully moist. This is quite an achievement, for so many meat loaves are good when hot, but tend to be dry and unappetising when cold. If freezing the loaf you can take out just the amount required, if you separate the slices as suggested under **Freezing** (below). If the loaf is for a picnic, carry it in its baking tin, if you need the whole amount.

Minced raw chicken could be used in the recipe instead of the minced beef.

FRUITED BEEF LOAF

25 g/1 oz butter or margarine
100 g/4 oz onion, finely chopped or grated
1 or 2 teaspoons curry powder, or to taste
300 ml/½ pint water
50 g/2 oz creamed coconut, cut into
    2.5 cm/1 inch pieces or 25 g/1 oz
    desiccated coconut
100 g/4 oz uncooked dried apricots, finely
    chopped
150 g/5 oz dessert apple, weight when
    peeled and finely chopped
2 tablespoons sultanas
1 tablespoon apricot or apple chutney
25 g/1 oz rolled oats
450 g/1 lb minced beef
salt and pepper
2 eggs
1 teaspoon corn oil

Preheat the oven to moderate (160°C, 325°F, Gas Mark 3). This is important for this recipe.

Heat the butter or margarine in a saucepan, add the onion; cook gently for a few minutes. Do not allow the onion to discolour. Blend the curry powder with the onion then pour in the water. Add the coconut and apricots. Stir over a low heat until the creamed coconut melts. Remove from the heat and allow the ingredients to stand for 5 minutes to soften the apricots slightly. Add the apple, sultanas, chutney and rolled oats; mix well. Stir in the meat with salt and pepper to taste. Beat very well to ensure there are no lumps of meat but a smooth mixture. Finally, mix in the eggs.

Use the oil to grease a 1 kg/2 lb loaf tin or line it with greaseproof paper and brush this with the oil. Spoon the meat mixture into the tin, smooth flat on top, but do not cover. Bake the loaf in the preheated oven for 1 hour 10 minutes.

To serve cold: Place greaseproof paper and a light weight over the top of the loaf and leave until cold.

To serve hot: Cool in the tin for 2 to 3 minutes before turning out.
Serves 6-8

For a special occasion, spread the top of the hot or cold loaf with a little chutney and top with sliced cucumber and sliced cooked apricots or tomato slices.
Barbecued Loaf: Cook the loaf and turn out on to a metal dish. Make the marinade as under Marinated Chops, page 107. Brush the loaf with this; heat over the barbecue.
Vegetarian Fruited Loaf: Omit the beef; use mashed cooked dried beans instead. You need 450 g/1 lb when cooked (p. 71).

FREEZING: Slice the loaf and insert a piece of greaseproof or waxed paper between the slices before freezing.

Fruited beef loaf (top right – recipe this page), Mixed bean salad (top left) and Stuffed barbecued herrings (recipes pages 106 and 107)

SUSTAINING SALADS

Each of the following salads would form a complete and very satisfying main course for a picnic or garden meal. The proportion of ingredients is very much a personal taste, so exact quantities are not given.

FISH AND RICE SALAD

Flake cooked fish: this could be all white fish or a mixture of white fish plus a few prawns, or a blend of white and smoked fish. Blend with cooked rice, cooked peas and a little grated raw carrot and diced red and green peppers. Add diced peeled cucumber and thin wedges of fresh tomatoes. Moisten the salad with a little oil and white wine vinegar or lemon juice then add enough mayonnaise or well-seasoned natural yogurt to make a fairly soft consistency.

Spoon on to a base of shredded lettuce or other salad greens. Top with finely chopped parsley and chives, or with chopped fennel leaves.

MEAT SALAD

Cut cooked meat into neat dice or, if the meat is already in thin slices, cut these into narrow strips. You could use all of one kind of meat, or mix ham or lamb with tongue; beef with ham; chicken with tongue or pork or salami; you can mix meat and cheese.

Blend the meat with diced cooked potatoes or cooked well drained macaroni (excellent cold in a salad). Add cooked diced carrots, chopped spring onions, cooked green beans and diced tomatoes. Blend with a mustard-flavoured mayonnaise or with a mixture of horseradish cream and natural yogurt.

This very 'robust' salad blends well with a base of shredded cabbage heart and finely chopped celery. Top the salad with stoned cooked prunes for an unexpected touch.

MIXED BEAN SALAD

This salad can be varied throughout the year. When fresh broad beans, runner beans or French beans are available, use some of these. Remember they should not be overcooked, for they continue softening a little as they cool. You could use frozen beans instead of fresh.

When the first broad beans come in season the pods are young and tender. These can be cooked, so you have two kinds of vegetable, the outer pods and the inner beans. Trim the pods, slice them (as though they were runner beans). Cook with the beans.

The bean salad looks attractive if you can mix three colours, for example, white butter beans, red kidney beans and green beans of some kind. There are directions for cooking dried beans on page 71.

For a dressing, blend 3 tablespoons oil, 1-1½ tablespoons lemon juice or white wine vinegar, 1 or 2 teaspoons chopped mint or savory (a delicious herb with beans) and a little seasoning.

Blend approximately 350 g/12 oz prepared beans with the dressing.

Line the base of the box in which the salad is being carried with crisp shredded lettuce, shredded cabbage heart or chopped Brussels sprouts, and spoon the bean mixture on top of the greens.

Serves 2-3

PLANNING A BARBECUE

Make sure the barbecue is well heated before you start to cook and do ensure that children are kept well away from the heat.

STUFFED BARBECUED HERRINGS

2 large fresh herrings
For the stuffing:
2 medium tomatoes, skinned and chopped
50 g/2 oz mushrooms, thinly sliced
1 tablespoon chopped chives or spring
  onions
salt and pepper
For the coating:
½ tablespoon corn oil
½ tablespoon lemon juice
teaspoon soy sauce

Ask the fishmonger to remove the heads from the fish and bone them. If this has not been done, it is not difficult to do yourself. First, cut away the heads with a sharp knife.

To bone herrings: Slit the fish along the stomach and remove the intestines, including the roes; save the roes. Turn the fish on to a board with the skin side uppermost. Run your forefinger firmly down the middle of each fish to loosen the backbone. Turn the fish over again and you will find you can easily lift the backbone and small bones away from the flesh.

Fill the fish with all the tomatoes, uncooked mushrooms, chives or spring onions and a very little seasoning. Fold the fish to enclose the stuffing, plus the roes.

Make 2 slits on each herring and lift on to a piece of oiled foil. Blend the corn oil, lemon juice and soy sauce. Spoon over the fish to coat it well.

Cook steadily over the barbecue fire or under a preheated grill for 10 to 15 minutes. If more convenient, bake in a moderate oven (180°C, 350°F, Gas Mark 4) for 25 minutes. Do not cover.

Serve with a mixed salad.

MICROWAVE: Place the fish on a flat plate. Allow approximately 7 minutes on **Full Power**.
NUTRITIONAL VALUE: Although herrings are an oily fish, this is not saturated fat.

MARINATED CHOPS

For the marinade:
1 medium onion, finely chopped or grated
2 garlic cloves, crushed
1 tablespoon corn oil
2 tablespoons chutney
2 tablespoons tomato ketchup
2 teaspoons Worcestershire sauce
2 teaspoons honey or brown sugar
1 tablespoon vinegar
3 tablespoons stock or cider
1 teaspoon made mustard
½ teaspoon curry powder

4 large lean lamb chops

Mix the ingredients for the marinade; pour into a shallow casserole. Add the lamb chops and leave for 2 to 3 hours. Turn over once or twice.

Lift out of the marinade and drain well. Cook the chops over the heated barbecue or under a preheated grill for 10 to 15 minutes. Turn the chops over once during cooking and brush with the marinade. Heat any marinade left and serve as a sauce.
Serves 4

PRACTICAL BAKING

This chapter covers a wide range of recipes for savoury and sweet biscuits, cakes and pastry dishes together with easy methods of making bread. Baking is a very satisfying form of cookery and home-baked foods are not only more appetising than those you buy but they can save you an appreciable amount of money.

As one gets older there is a tendency to eat rather less at main meals and to supplement these with small snacks in between. It is really quite a good idea to eat 'little and often', provided the snacks consist of nutritious and not over-sweet or over-fatty foods, so a well-filled biscuit tin is a great asset.

Creaming fat and sugar, or rubbing fat into flour is very easy when one is young, but it can become more difficult for some older people, who may suffer from stiffer wrists and fingers. If you do an appreciable amount of baking it is certainly worthwhile investing in an electric mixer or food processor to carry out these functions. Softer-type fats are also an asset when using the one-stage process.

If you have been advised to limit the intake of fat in your diet or to buy polyunsaturated fats and oils, you will find here recipes that make the best use of these ingredients. There are several cake recipes that do not need eggs.

The section ends with some suggestions on baking for special functions, such as a charity bazaar. The dishes would be equally suitable for those happy occasions when the family come to visit you, or you plan a large gathering for teatime at home.

Although most of the recipes are created for use in a conventional oven there are several dishes which are equally good if a microwave cooker is used (see page 113).

Oaties (top), and Orange oaty cookies, Bran biscuits and Rolled oat macaroons (on the large plate – recipes pages 110 and 111)

BAKING THE NEW WAY

There is no doubt you will have favourite recipes that you have used successfully for many years. In this section, therefore, I have concentrated on a rather new approach to baking. I have included those foods that come under the heading of 'being good for us', like bran, rolled oats and wholemeal flour. I have, however, made absolutely certain that the recipes produce delicious food.

Good biscuits
Many commercially made biscuits are disappointing in flavour as well as being really very expensive. The recipes that follow are full of food value and easy to make.

Always store biscuits in a really 100% airtight tin away from cakes or pastry. They will keep beautifully crisp. If biscuits are a little soft after baking, or in storage, bake again for a short time. The word 'biscuit' means 'double or twice baked'.

BRAN BISCUITS

75 g/ 3 oz butter or margarine
50 g/2 oz soft brown sugar
1 level tablespoon malt extract
1 tablespoon golden syrup
50 g/2 oz bran
40 g/1½ oz rolled oats
40 g/ 1½ oz wholemeal plain flour

Lightly grease 2 flat baking sheets. Preheat the oven to moderate (160°C, 325°F, Gas Mark 3) while cutting or shaping the biscuits.

Cream the butter or margarine and sugar, malt and syrup. Add the bran, rolled oats and flour and knead the mixture well.

As this mixture is crumbly it is easier to roll it out between two sheets of greaseproof paper to about 6 mm/¼ inch thick then cut it into about 14 rounds. If you find this troublesome, make the mixture into 14 small balls and press these out into neat rounds with the palms of your hands.

Arrange on the two greased baking sheets, allowing room for them to spread out slightly. Put in the preheated oven and bake for 20 minutes, or until firm around the edges. Allow to cool for several minutes on the baking sheets before lifting them off on to a wire tray.
Makes 14

VARIATIONS:
Use ½ tablespoon malt and 1½ tablespoons golden syrup.
Use 40 g/1½ oz bran and 50 g/2 oz wholemeal flour.

WATER BISCUITS

225 g /8 oz plain white flour
½ teaspoon salt
25–40 g/1-1½ oz margarine
water to bind

Sift the flour and salt, rub in the margarine. Gradually add enough water to make a firm rolling consistency. Roll out to an oblong. Fold in 3 like an envelope; turn and roll out again until paper thin then cut into neat squares.

While rolling and cutting the dough preheat the oven to very hot (230°C, 450°F, Gas Mark 8). It must be very hot when the biscuits are cooked. Put the biscuits on to ungreased baking sheets. Bake towards the top of the oven for 3 to 4 minutes until crisp and golden.
Makes about 36

OATIES

75 g/3 oz butter or margarine
25 g/1 oz caster sugar
175 g/6 oz plain wholemeal or wheatmeal
  flour
1/4 teaspoon salt
50 g/2 oz rolled oats
milk to bind

Preheat the oven to moderate (160°C, 325°F, Gas Mark 3).

Cream together the butter or margarine and sugar until soft. Sift the flour and salt into the creamed mixture, add the rolled oats then knead well. Gradually blend in milk to make a firm rolling consistency.

Place on a lightly floured board and roll out until 6 mm/1/4 inch thick. Cut into 15–18 rounds. Place on lightly greased baking sheets. Prick lightly with a fork.

Bake in the centre of the preheated oven for 15 minutes or until firm. As the oaties are very brittle, allow them to cool for 10 minutes or until firm. Then remove on to a wire cooling tray.
Makes 15–18

ORANGE OATY COOKIES

100 g /4 oz butter or margarine
75 g/3 oz caster sugar
2 teaspoons finely grated orange rind
100 g/4 oz plain white or brown flour
50 g /2 oz rolled oats
approximately 1 tablespoon orange juice

Cream the butter or margarine with half the sugar and the orange rind until soft and light. Add the flour and rolled oats and mix well, then gradually blend in the juice. Knead then wrap and chill for 1 hour.

Preheat the oven to moderate (180°C, 350°F, Gas Mark 4).

Roll out the dough until 6 mm/1/4 inch thick then cut into 7 cm/2½ inch rounds. Put the remaining sugar on a large plate and press each biscuit round into the sugar until lightly coated on either side.

Put the biscuits on to ungreased baking sheets and cook for approximately 12 minutes, or until firm. Allow to cool before removing from the baking sheets.
Makes 12–14

VARIATION:
Use lemon rind and juice in place of orange rind and juice.

ROLLED OAT MACAROONS

75 g/3 oz margarine
50 g/2 oz caster sugar
few drops vanilla or almond essence
1 level tablespoon golden syrup
100 g/4 oz self-raising or plain flour sifted
  with 1 teaspoon baking powder
100 g/4 oz rolled oats

Preheat the oven to moderate (180°C, 350°F, Gas Mark 4).

Cream the margarine with the sugar, essence and golden syrup until soft. Gradually blend in the flour, or flour and baking powder, and rolled oats. Knead well.

Divide the mixture into 16 portions; roll into balls. Place sheets of rice paper on 2 large baking sheets or trays; arrange the biscuits on the paper, allowing plenty of space for them to spread.

Bake for 15 to 20 minute in the centre of the oven. When nearly cold, cut or tear away the surplus rice paper.
Makes 16

NOTE: if no rice paper is available put the biscuits on greased trays.

CAKES WITHOUT EGGS

These recipes enable you to enjoy eggless cakes. Brown (often called wheatmeal) flour can be used in these recipes.

BOILED FRUIT CAKE

300 ml/½ pint fairly strong tea (see method)
100 g/4 oz margarine
100 g/4 oz moist brown sugar
100–175 g/4–6 oz dried fruit
300 g/10 oz self-raising white or brown flour
  or plain flour sifted with 2½ teaspoons
  baking powder
½ teaspoon bicarbonate of soda
1 teaspoon mixed spice

The tea should be made in the usual way, allowed to stand for about 3 minutes then carefully strained. Line a 20 cm/8 inch cake tin with greased greaseproof paper. Even if using a silicone 'non-stick' tin, it is advisable to grease and flour the inside for the high proportion of liquid in this recipe is inclined to make the cake stick.

Pour the tea into a good-sized saucepan, add the margarine, sugar and dried fruit. Bring the tea to boiling point; boil for 1 minute and then allow to become cold.

Meanwhile, preheat the oven to moderately hot (190°C, 375°F, Gas Mark 5).

Sift the dry ingredients into the saucepan, mix very thoroughly then spoon into the prepared tin. Bake in the centre of the oven for 1 hour, or until firm.
Serves 6–8

FREEZING: This freezes well.

GOLDEN SPONGE

85 g*/3 oz margarine
85 g*/3 oz caster sugar
1 level tablespoon golden syrup**
175 g/6 oz self-raising white or brown flour
  sifted with 1 teaspoon baking powder or
  plain flour sifted with 2½ teaspoons
  baking powder
150 ml/¼ pint skimmed milk
* use this metrication, i.e. a generous 75 g
** measure this carefully

Grease and flour or line 2 × 16.5–18 cm/6½–7 inch sandwich tins. Preheat the oven to moderately hot (180–190°C, 350–375°F, Gas Mark 4–5). Use the lower setting if your oven tends to be fierce in heat.

Cream the margarine, sugar and golden syrup until soft and light. Fold the flour and baking powder and milk alternately into the mixture. Spoon into the prepared tins and bake for 18 minutes, or until firm to the touch. This sponge can be filled with jam or with fruit and whipped cream.
Serves 4

VARIATIONS:
For a thicker sponge, as illustrated, increase the ingredients by 50 per cent, i.e. use 125 g/4½ oz margarine etc. Bake in a 19 cm/7½ inch tin for 25 minutes.
Chocolate Sponge: Omit 25 g/1 oz flour and use 25 g/1 oz cocoa. Do not increase the amount of baking powder but you may add an extra 25 g/1 oz sugar.
Coffee Sponge: Use half moderately strong coffee and half milk instead of all milk. You may like to increase the amount of sugar by 25 g/1 oz.
Ginger Sponge: Add 1–1½ teaspoons ground ginger to the flour.
Iced Sponge: Any of these cakes can be topped with glacé icing (see page 136).

APPLE SAUCE CAKE

*250 ml/8 fl oz thick unsweetened apple
    purée (see method)*
100 g/4 oz margarine
150 g/5 oz light brown sugar
100–175 g/4–6 oz dried fruit
*225 g/8 oz self-raising flour sifted with 1
    teaspoon baking powder or plain flour
    sifted with 3 teaspoons baking powder*
2 tablespoons milk or juice (see method)

The apple purée must be prepared first to give it time to become cold. The way to obtain a really thick purée is to bake 2 medium-sized cooking apples in the oven or microwave cooker (see page 76), then scoop out the pulp. If you have stewed the apples the mixture must be well strained through a sieve. In this case, you could use the juice instead of the milk.

Line the base of a 19–20 cm/7½–8 inch tin with greased greaseproof paper; grease and flour the sides. Preheat the oven to moderate (180°C, 350°F, Gas Mark 4).

Cream the margarine and sugar until soft and light, add the apple purée, dried fruit, flour and milk alternately (or use the All-in-One Method given on page 125).

Spoon into the tin and bake for 50 to 60 minutes, or until firm to touch. This cake is nicer if very slightly sticky.
Serves 6

VARIATIONS:
Orange or Lemon Apple Cake: Add 1 teaspoon grated lemon or orange rind and use the fruit juice instead of milk to mix.
Spiced Apple Cake: Add ½ to 1 teaspoon ground cloves or ground cinnamon.
MICROWAVE: Use a dish the same size as the tin. Cook for 10 minutes on **Roast** setting or 8½–9 minutes on **Full Power**.

MICROWAVE CAKES

With a combination cooker you have the facilities of true baking but in the case of an ordinary microwave cooker I feel it better to use recipes with an appreciable amount of liquid, rather than trying to achieve a comparable result with baking in the case of classic recipes, like a Victoria sandwich, which become very like a steamed sponge.

Golden sponge in a microwave
Line the base of a 19–20 cm/7½–8 inch soufflé dish or similar container which must be at least 7.5 cm/3 inch deep (for cakes rise drastically in a microwave cooker), with a round of lightly greased greaseproof paper. Lightly grease the sides of the dish. No cover is needed when cooking cakes.

Make the sponge as the recipe and spoon into the dish. Bake for approximately 8 minutes on **Roast** setting or 7 minutes on **Full Power**. Test, as method below. Allow to stand for some minutes then turn out.

Both the Gingerbread recipe on page 125 and the Apple sauce cake, left, are good recipes for microwave cooking.

To test the cake: Insert a fine wooden cocktail stick; if it comes out clean the cake is cooked and any stickiness will go as it stands.

Problems may arise: If the base of the cake is slightly sticky, when the rest is cooked perfectly, simply stand the dish on an upturned saucer next time you cook a cake. This problem arises in some cookers.

If the cake looks to be rising unevenly during cooking, turn the dish round every 2 minutes.

DESSERT CAKES

It is a good idea to make some cakes that can 'double up' as desserts.

Fill part of the Golden Sponge on page 113 or Crunchy Shortcake below with fruit, the rest with jam. Several cakes here are delicious hot with golden syrup or apple or custard sauces.

DATE AND GINGER CAKE

75 g/3 oz margarine or cooking fat
50 g/2 oz light brown sugar
2 tablespoons golden syrup
100 g/4 oz cooking dates, chopped
200 g/7 oz self-raising flour or plain flour
*   sifted with 1¾ teaspoons baking powder*
1 teaspoon ground ginger
½ teaspoon bicarbonate of soda
3 tablespoons milk
1 egg

Line a tin, measuring approximately 18 × 25 cm/7 × 10 inches with greased greaseproof paper. Preheat the oven to moderate (160°C, 325°F, Gas Mark 3).

Heat the margarine or fat with the sugar and syrup over a low heat until the sugar has melted. Add the dates to the hot mixture, allow to cool. Sift the flour with the ginger and bicarbonate of soda. Add the melted ingredients and stir briskly. Heat the milk in the saucepan, stir to make sure no sugar etc. is wasted. Pour over the other ingredients. Add the egg and mix well.

Spoon the mixture into the lined tin and bake in the preheated oven for about 50 minutes, or until firm to the touch. Allow to cool for 20 minutes before turning on to a cake rack.

STREUSEL CAKES

This term describes a cake with a crisp crumble top. The following makes a topping for the Boiled fruit cake (page 112) or the Apple sauce cake (page 113).

Melt 40 g/1½ oz butter or margarine, mix in 50 g/2 oz Demerara sugar, 50 g/2oz chopped walnuts, 50 g/2 oz rolled oats or wholemeal flour and about ½ teaspoon ground cinnamon.

Sprinkle over the cake mixture before baking. Allow an extra 5 minutes' cooking.

CRUNCHY SHORTCAKE

50 g/2 oz margarine
175 g/6 oz self-raising flour or plain flour
*   sifted with 1½ teaspoons baking powder*
50 g/2 oz caster or granulated sugar
50 g/2 oz toasted oats, crushed cornflakes
*   or other breakfast cereal*
1 egg or extra milk
milk to mix

Lightly grease 1 or 2 baking sheets. Preheat the oven to moderately hot (200°C, 400°F, Gas Mark 6).

Rub the margarine into the flour or flour and baking powder, add the sugar, oats or cereal, the egg and just enough milk to make a scone-like consistency. Divide the dough into 2 equal parts. Pat or roll out each piece until about 18 cm/7 inch in diameter. Put on to the tray or trays. Bake in the preheated oven for nearly 20 minutes, or until golden brown and crisp.

Allow to cool then fill with seasonal fruit and whipped cream or thick natural yogurt.

Golden sponge (top) and Boiled fruit cake (recipes page 112)

EASY BREAD MAKING

The essential ingredient for 'proper' bread is yeast. There have been new developments in the field of bread making. Packets of bread mix with the right proportions of yeast and flour are now available. You can also obtain dried fast-acting yeast, which cuts down on a lot of the time as only one, instead of two, proving periods are required. The method of using the yeast is simple, too, in that you mix it with the flour.

The proportions given are based upon using a full packet of this fast yeast plus 750 g/1½ lb flour. This amount, and the weight of water, produces 3 small loaves.

If you want to make a real batch of several loaves using a full packet, i.e. 1.5 kg/3.3 lb flour, you then need 2 packets of this particular yeast.

The ideal flour for bread making is called 'strong'. This gives a better texture and improves the quality of the rising. If your store has no strong flour, then you can use plain flour.

QUICK METHOD

1 packet fast-action yeast
750 g/1 lb 11 oz (half a bag) of strong white or brown or wholemeal flour
up to 2 level teaspoons salt (to taste)
25 g/1 oz margarine or butter or lard or 1 tablespoon oil
white flour – 450 ml/¾ pint (15 fl oz) water
brown flour – 450 ml/¾ pint (15 fl oz) plus 2 tablespoons water
wholemeal flour – 525 ml/17½ fl oz water

Mix the yeast, flour and salt; rub in the margarine or other fat or add the oil. Heat the water until pleasantly warm (if you use 1 part boiling water and 2 parts cold water you achieve the right temperature for this particular type of yeast).

Turn the dough on to a lightly floured surface; knead well. To do this by hand, fold the dough toward you then push it away. Continue doing this, using the base of the palm (known as the 'heel' of your hand). The dough is ready when it feels firm but elastic and is no longer sticky. It takes about 10 minutes.

This process can be done in an electric mixer or food processor; check the progress continually for over-kneading is as bad as under-kneading.

To test if the dough is sufficiently kneaded, press it with a floured finger. If the impression comes out, the dough is ready for shaping.

Shaping the dough
Divide the dough into 2 or 3 portions. The easiest shape to make is a 'cob'. Form each portion into a neat round; put on to lightly greased and warmed baking sheets or trays. Make a deep cross or other design on the top with a floured knife.

To make tin loaves, lightly grease 3 × 450 g/1 lb loaf tins. Press the dough out to form 3 neat oblongs the length and 3 times the width of the tins. Fold the dough neatly to fit the tins, with the fold underneath.

You can, of course, make 3 different sorts of loaf or some loaves and some rolls.

'Proving' the dough
Place lightly oiled clingfilm gently over the loaves or the tins; allow room for the dough to rise. The clingfilm prevents an unwanted skin forming. You can choose just how you will let the dough rise to fit in with your

plans. The dough is ready to cook when it has almost doubled in size; do not let it go on rising after this stage. The times below apply to this type of yeast mixture.

Quick rise, in a warm kitchen or airing cupboard – from 45 minutes to 1 hour.

Microwave rise, takes a certain amount of practice but shortens the time by half. The dough must be put into microwave ware, not tins. Allow approximately 15 seconds on **Full Power**, then let the dough stand for up to 10 minutes. Repeat until risen.

Slower rise, 2 hours in a cool place or up to 24 hours in the storage compartment *not the freezing* compartment of the refrigerator. After this the dough must stand at room temperature for 20 minutes before baking.

Baking the bread
If baking 3 small loaves or trays of rolls, preheat the oven to very hot (230°C, 450°F, Gas Mark 8). With 2 larger loaves you can bake at this temperature and reduce it slightly after 25 minutes or you could cook the whole time in a hot oven (220°C, 425°F, Gas Mark 7).

Allow approximately 30 minutes' cooking time for the smaller loaves or, if baking 2 slightly larger loaves, allow 35 to 40 minutes. To test if cooked, knock each loaf on the bottom; they should sound hollow.

VARIATIONS:
In each case the variations are based upon using the same amount of yeast etc.
Bran Bread: Allow 100 g/4 oz bran; reduce the amount of flour by 100 g/4 oz.
Cheese Bread: Sift a little pepper and dry mustard powder with the flour. Add 100 g/4 oz grated cheese before adding the liquid.
Fruit Bread: Add 100 g/4 oz dried fruit.
Herbed Bread: Add 2 tablespoons chopped herbs e.g. parsley, chives, or peeled and crushed garlic cloves.
Milk Bread: Mix the dough with skimmed milk instead of water.
Oat Bread: Allow 525 g/1 lb 3 oz flour and 225 g/8 oz rolled oats.
Pizza: Use ⅓ of the dough after kneading or ⅙th of the dough if basing recipe on a full bag of flour and 2 packets of yeast. If making specially use 225 g/8 oz flour and ⅓ packet of yeast. See directions, page 103.
Poppy Seed Bread: Brush the loaves with milk or egg after proving: top with poppy seeds.
Rolls: Use 50 g/2 oz kneaded dough for good-sized rolls; less for smaller ones. Form into shapes, put on to lightly greased baking sheets. Cover lightly with oiled clingfilm; allow to prove for 30 to 35 minutes in a warm place. Brush with a little milk or egg. Cook for 12 to 15 minutes in a very hot oven (230°C, 450°F, Gas Mark 8).

Making bread the traditional way
To the 750 g/1 lb 11 oz flour add the same amount of salt, fat and liquid as the recipe; but allow 20 g/¾ oz fresh yeast or ¾ level tablespoon (11 g) ordinary dried yeast.

Cream fresh yeast, add the tepid liquid then blend with the flour etc. If using dried yeast first dissolve 1 to 2 teaspoons sugar or honey in the tepid liquid; sprinkle the yeast on top. Wait for 10 minutes, mix well then proceed as for fresh yeast.

You then knead the dough as before until smooth. You must allow this to prove in bulk until double its original size. After this you knead it again (called 'knocking back') then form into the required shapes. Prove for the second time as the timing in this recipe. Bake the bread as in the recipe.

If using a 1.5 kg/3.3 lb bag of flour use double the amounts of liquid, fat and salt but increase fresh yeast to 25 g/1 oz and dried yeast to 1 tablespoon (15 g/½ oz).

MORE IDEAS WITH YEAST

The simple buns below are exactly like bread and would be extremely popular with hungry children. They are very inexpensive to make.

The Christmas bread would be a great success for a Special Christmas Fayre or Bazaar; it is cheaper to make than a cake.

CHRISTMAS BREAD

15 g/½ oz fresh yeast or ½ tablespoon
* dried yeast (or see Variation, below)*
150 ml/¼ pint water plus 2 tablespoons
50 g/2 oz sugar
350 g/12 oz plain white flour
pinch salt
50 g/ 2 oz margarine
½–1 teaspoon caraway seeds
150 g/5 oz mixed dried fruit
75 g/3 oz candied peel, chopped
1 egg

Cream the fresh yeast; warm the water, add to the yeast.

If using dried yeast, warm the water, add 2 teaspoons of the sugar then sprinkle the dried yeast on top. Allow to stand for 10 minutes, mix and use as fresh yeast.

Sift the flour and salt, rub in the margarine, add the remaining sugar, seeds and yeast liquid, and mix well. Add the dried fruit and peel then the egg. Mix with a knife then knead well. Continue kneading until smooth, as the method given on page 116. Cover and prove for about 1½ to 2 hours, or until double in size. Knead again and form into a 20 cm/8 inch round or place into a greased and floured cake tin which is the same diameter.

Cover and prove for approximately 30 minutes or until well risen. Meanwhile, preheat the oven to hot (220°C, 425°F, Gas Mark 7). Bake for 20 minutes at this temperature then lower the heat to 180–190°C, 350–375°F, Gas Mark 4–5, and cook for a further 20 minutes.
Serves 8

VARIATION:
If using the fast-acting yeast described on page 116, use a whole packet; this compensates for the extra weight of fat, fruit, etc. Add to the flour, then incorporate the other ingredients. Knead well, form into the round and allow to prove. This may well take longer than 30 minutes for it is the only proving time. Bake as above.

BUNS WITH YEAST

The great advantage of a yeast dough for simple buns is that these are economical so are ideal for hungry youngsters or for a charity bazaar. You can use the basic bread dough on pages 116 and 117. Take off a little and use it to make:–

Devonshire Splits: Form the dough into rounds, prove and bake as the Rolls on page 117. When cold, split and fill with jam and whipped cream. Top with icing sugar.

Swiss Buns: Form the dough into finger shapes; prove and bake as the Rolls on page 117. When cold, top with Glacé icing.

FREEZING: Freeze the baked buns for up to 1 month then defrost and fill or decorate.

Fine home-made bread – white poppy seed bread and rolls (recipe pages 116–117)

IRISH SODA BREAD

This lovely light bread is made without yeast; do not exceed the recommended amount of bicarbonate of soda. Remember all spoon measures should be level.

450 g/1 lb plain white, brown (often known as wheatmeal) or wholemeal flour
½ to 1 teaspoon salt
½ teaspoon bicarbonate of soda
½ teaspoon cream of tartar (see Variation)
300 ml/½ pint buttermilk with white flour
300 ml/½ pint buttermilk plus 1 tablespoon with brown flour
300 ml/½ pint buttermilk plus 2 tablespoons with wholemeal flour

Sift the dry ingredients together; gradually add the buttermilk. The amount given should produce a soft dough but one that can be kneaded, but makes of flour vary slightly in the amount of liquid they absorb. Turn on to a lightly floured surface and knead for a minute or two.

Preheat the oven to hot (220°C, 425°F, Gas Mark 7).

To bake: Make into 1 or 2 rounds of about 2.5–3.5 cm/1–1½ inches thick. Put on to a lightly floured baking sheet. (Greasing is rarely necessary for this type of bread.) Put in the preheated oven. One larger loaf takes approximately 30 minutes and the smaller ones about 25 minutes. Check after 15 minutes and reduce the heat slightly if the bread is becoming too brown.

To cook on a griddle: If you have a griddle tucked away, use this as it saves heating the oven. Make 1 or 2 rounds about 2 cm/¾ inch thick. Heat, but do not grease the griddle. To test the heat, shake on a little flour. It should turn golden in 1 to 1½ minutes. Put the round or rounds on the griddle. Cook for 5 to 7 minutes, turn over with a fish slice and cook for the same time on the second side.

Test the bread by knocking on the bottom: it should sound hollow.

VARIATION:
Buttermilk is not always obtainable; you can use skimmed milk plus an extra ½ teaspoon cream of tartar.

SCONES

225 g/8 oz white, brown or wholemeal self-raising flour or plain flour sifted with 2 teaspoons baking powder
pinch salt
25–40 g/1–1½ oz margarine
milk to mix

Home-made scones are infinitely better than those you buy and can be served at coffee or tea-time. They freeze well.

The secret is to have the oven really well preheated and the dough fairly soft. Preheat the oven to hot (220°C, 425°F, Gas Mark 7).

Sift the flour and salt, rub in the margarine and add enough milk to make a soft rolling consistency. Roll out until between 1.5–2 cm/½–¾ inch thick. Cut into rounds or triangles. Put on an ungreased baking sheet. Bake for 10 to 12 minutes or until the sides are firm to gentle pressure.
Makes 14–16

VARIATIONS:
Oatmeal Scones: Use 175 g/6 oz flour and 50 g/ 2 oz rolled oats plus an extra ½ teaspoon baking powder.
Savoury Scones: Add seasoning and 50 g/ 2 oz grated cheese to the flour and fat.
Sweet Scones: Add 25–50 g/1–2 oz sugar to the scone dough with up 75 g/3 oz dried fruit such as sultanas.

SHORTCRUST PASTRY

The traditional method of making this pastry is to sift 225 g/8 oz plain flour with a pinch of salt then rub in 110 g/4 oz fat. i.e. half fat to flour (the slightly unusual metrication gives this: just weigh out a generous 100 g).

The pastry is then bound with water, or an alternative, as given below, then gathered into a ball and rolled out on a lightly floured surface.

While you can use soft polyunsaturated margarine or soft fat in this method of making pastry, the One-Stage or All-in-One Method on the right is recommended.

Freezing pastry

Cooked or uncooked pastry made in any of the ways given above or on the right, freezes well. If preparing shortcrust specially for the freezer, mix the pastry with milk, rather than water. It keeps a better texture. Shape uncooked pastry into a shallow oblong then wrap.

Flavouring pastry

Shortcrust pastry can be adapted in many ways including:
Cheese Pastry: Season the flour with salt, a shake of pepper and pinch of dry mustard powder. Add 50 g/2 oz finely grated cheese. This pastry is often bound with egg yolk and water.
Sweet Shortcrust Pastry: Add 25–50 g/1–2 oz caster or sifted icing sugar to the flour in the All-in-One or Oil methods; with the usual rubbed-in method, add to the fat and flour mixture.

This pastry is generally bound with an egg yolk as well as a little water.

Making a flan shape

Roll out the pastry and line the recommended size tin or dish or a flan ring on an upturned baking tray (this makes it easier to remove than when dealing with the rim). Often the flan is baked 'blind', i.e. before filling. Fill the pastry with foil or greaseproof paper and crusts of bread or plastic baking beans to keep the base flat. Bake as the recipe.

ALL-IN-ONE METHOD

225 g/8 oz plain flour (see page 122)
pinch salt
110 g/4 oz polyunsaturated margarine or soft fat
3 tablespoons water

Sift the flour and salt into a basin. Put the margarine or other fat into a mixing bowl, add the water plus 2 tablespoons of the flour. Cream this mixture well then gradually work in the rest of the flour.

VARIATION:
Use 150 g/5 oz margarine and only 2 tablespoons water.

PASTRY WITH OIL

Choose a polyunsaturated oil (see page 128 for varieties).

225 g/8 oz plain flour
pinch salt
120 ml/4 fl oz (6 tablespoons) oil
1 tablespoon water

Sift the flour and salt into a bowl; add the oil and water, blend together then roll out.

This pastry is difficult to handle and is better rolled out between sheets of greaseproof paper.

NEW WAYS IN PASTRY

As pastry has been a traditional food for a very long time, it may seem strange to consider new methods of making it. There are, however, important changes in the ingredients we are recommended to include in our modern diet. It is possible to incorporate some of these into pastry.

Choice of flour

While it is possible to make shortcrust pastry entirely with wholemeal flour, a lighter result is achieved by using half plain white flour and half plain wholemeal flour. This produces pastry that is easy to handle and which has a pleasantly 'nutty' taste. If you decide to use all wholemeal flour you may prefer the pastry made with self-raising, rather than plain, flour. Although modern wholemeal flour has a fine texture, the pastry can be difficult to roll out, as it tends to crumble easily. You can overcome this by rolling the pastry between sheets of greaseproof paper.

Brown flour, often called wheatmeal flour, which has slightly less fibre than wholemeal flour, can also be used for pastry.

You can use 175 g/6 oz flour plus 50 g/2 oz rolled oats instead of 225 g/8 oz flour.

Choice of fat

In the past butter, lard, special pastry cooking fat and firm margarine were used in making pastry. You can still choose these but all are high in saturated fats. Try making shortcrust pastry with one of the polyunsaturated margarines or special white fats or polyunsaturated oil, as methods on page 121.

ORANGE CRUMB TART

Sweet shortcrust pastry made with 100 g/
*   4 oz flour etc. (see page 121)*
For the filling:
1 small orange
3 tablespoons orange marmalade
50 g/2 oz butter or margarine
50 g/2 oz caster sugar
1 egg
50 g/2 oz self-raising flour or plain flour
*   sifted with ½ teaspoon baking powder*
50 g/2 oz soft breadcrumbs

Preheat the oven to moderately hot (190–200°C, 375–400°F, Gas Mark 5–6). Roll out the pastry and line an 18 cm/7 inch flan dish or tin or flan ring.

Finely grate the 'zest' (top orange part of the rind) from the fruit; halve the fruit and squeeze out enough juice to give 1 tablespoon. Spread the pastry with half the marmalade; put the remainder into a mixing bowl and cream with the butter or margarine and sugar. Add the egg and beat well then blend in the flour, or flour and baking powder, and crumbs. Finally add the orange juice.

Spoon into the pastry case and bake for 15 minutes in the centre of the preheated oven then lower the heat to moderate (180°C, 350°F, Gas Mark 4) and bake for a further 15 minutes. Serve hot or cold.
Serves 4

VARIATION:
Iced Orange Crumb Tart: Allow tart to become cold. Blend 75 g/3 oz icing sugar with a little orange juice; spread over the top of the tart. Allow to set.

FREEZING: This tart freezes very well.

Making Sweet shortcrust pastry for a fruit pie
(pastry recipe page 121)

BAKING FOR BAZAARS

Although this heading assumes you will be baking for a good cause, you will find the recipes equally suitable for entertaining friends and family. Several of the cakes or pastries are baked in large oblong tins; this means they can be cut into fingers, to be sold individually. All the recipes freeze well and the individual portions defrost very quickly.

CHERRY ALMOND SLICES

Sweet shortcrust pastry made with 175 g/ 6 oz flour (see page 121)
For the filling:
3 tablespoons cherry jam
2 egg whites
few drops almond essence
100 g/4 oz ground almonds or 50 g/2 oz ground almonds and 50 g/2 oz fine sponge crumbs
75 g /3 oz caster sugar
50 g/2 oz glacé cherries, chopped

Preheat the oven to moderately hot (190°C, 375°F, Gas Mark 5).

Roll out the pastry and line a Swiss roll tin measuring approximately 27 × 18 cm/ 11 × 7 inches. Spread the jam over the pastry. Whisk the egg whites until frothy, add the almond essence, ground almonds, or ground almonds and crumbs. Mix well then stir in the sugar and cherries. Spread over the pastry base and bake in the preheated oven for 30–35 minutes. Mark into fingers while warm and remove from the tin.
Makes 16

SCOTCH SHORTBREAD

100 g/4 oz plain flour
50 g/2 oz ground rice or rice flour or cornflour
100 g/4 oz butter
50 g/2 oz caster sugar
extra caster sugar

Preheat the oven to cool (150°C, 300°F, Gas Mark 2).

Sift the dry ingredients into a bowl. Dice the butter, rub into the flour mixture. Add the sugar; knead until smooth. Form into a neat shape, about 1.5 cm/½ inch thick, on an ungreased baking sheet. Flute the edges.

Bake in the centre of the preheated oven for 35 to 40 minutes until very firm, but still pale. Mark into 8 triangles; cool on the baking sheet. Top with caster sugar.
Makes 8

VICTORIA SANDWICH

175g/ 6 oz butter or margarine
175 g/6 oz caster sugar
3 large eggs, well beaten
175 g/6 oz self-raising white or brown flour or plain flour sifted with 1½ teaspoons baking powder

Grease and flour 2 × 19–20 cm/7½–8 inch sandwich tins. Pre-heat the oven to moderate (180°C, 350°F, Gas Mark 4). In some ovens you may need 190°C, 375°F, Gas Mark 5.

Cream the butter or margarine and sugar until soft and light. Gradually beat the eggs into the creamed mixture. If this shows signs of curdling, beat in a little of the flour. Sift the flour, or flour and baking powder; fold this gently but thoroughly into the creamed mixture. Spoon into the tins; smooth flat on top.

Bake for 20 minutes, or until firm to a gentle touch. Cool in the tins for a minute then carefully turn out.

When cold, sandwich the sponges with jam. Top with caster sugar.
Serves 6–8

VARIATION:
All-in-One Method: If you use soft margarine or allow harder fats to soften at room temperature, you can put all the ingredients into a bowl. Cream for 2 minutes by hand or allow 1 minute in an electric mixer or ½ minute in a food processor.

GINGERBREAD

110 g*/4 oz margarine
110 g*/4 oz moist brown sugar
175 g/6 oz black treacle or golden syrup
225 g/8 oz plain white or brown flour
2 teaspoons ground ginger
½ teaspoon bicarbonate of soda
4 tablespoons milk
1 egg
½ teaspoon grated lemon rind
* use this metrication

Line a 15 × 20 cm/6 × 8 inch tin with greased greaseproof paper. Preheat the oven to moderate (160°C, 325°F, Gas Mark 3).

Heat the margarine, sugar and treacle or syrup in a saucepan or bowl in the microwave until the fat has melted. Sift the flour and ginger, add the melted ingredients, mix well.

Stir the bicarbonate of soda into 1 tablespoon of the milk; heat the rest of the milk in the pan or bowl. Beat all the ingredients together. Pour into the prepared tin. Bake in the preheated oven for 50 to 60 minutes, until firm to a gentle touch. Cool in the tin.
Serves 8

RAISIN BARS

For the biscuit dough:
225 g/8 oz plain flour
1 teaspoon baking powder
pinch salt
100 g/4 oz butter or margarine
100 g/4 oz caster sugar
½ teaspoon vanilla essence
1 egg
2 tablespoons milk
For the topping:
225 g/8 oz seedless raisins
150 ml/¼ pint water
½ teaspoon ground ginger
1 teaspoon arrowroot or cornflour
2 tablespoons lemon juice
75 g/3 oz brown sugar
50 g/2 oz mixed candied peel, finely chopped

Sift the flour, baking powder and salt together. Cream the butter or margarine with the sugar and vanilla essence, beat in the egg, add the flour and milk. Mix together and knead lightly. Chill if sticky.

Meanwhile, heat the raisins, water and ginger in a pan for 5 minutes, until the raisins are plump. Blend the arrowroot or cornflour with the lemon juice, add to the ingredients in the pan with the sugar. Stir over a low heat until thickened then cool.

Preheat the oven to moderately hot (190°C, 375°F, Gas Mark 5).

Roll out two-thirds of the dough and use to line the base and sides of a 20 cm/8 inch square sandwich tin. Top with the raisin mixture. Roll out the remaining dough until 3 mm/⅛th inch thick, cut into 1.5 cm/½ inch strips. Arrange in a lattice design over the filling. Bake in the centre of the preheated oven for 30 minutes. Cut into fingers while warm.
Make 16

HEALTH-GIVING FOODS

Good health is a priceless possession and anything one can do to maintain this is worth considering. Nowadays it has been proved conclusively that the right choice of food can make an important contribution towards good health at any age.

It is wise therefore for people to learn a little of the function of foods and to make adjustments in their diet if they feel, or have been advised, this is necessary. In order to check that your meals really are well balanced the following pages give information about the function of various foods.

Sometimes, so much stress is laid upon what one should, or should not, eat that there may be a tendency to feel that the food which promotes good health is not necessarily interesting or appetising. That, of course, is quite wrong. It is perfectly possible to eat delicious meals which are also ideal from a nutritional standpoint.

During recent years there has been considerable research into the part food plays in maintaining good health. Certain clear guide lines have been given us by the medical profession.

It is recommended that we try to avoid being overweight, for this can be a contributing factor in heart disease and hypertension (high blood pressure). People who are overweight tend to suffer arthritis and rheumatism more severely than those who remain slim.

In the past it was believed that as people got older it was normal to put on weight. If we take reasonable exercise and eat sensibly our weight should remain stable. Eating sensibly does not mean depriving ourselves of good meals but rather choosing food wisely and avoiding overeating. If you are seriously overweight now you should seek medical advice.

Fresh fruit and vegetables, essential parts of a healthy, balanced diet

FOOD AND HEALTH

Certain medical and health problems affect many people as they become older.

Hypertension

This means that blood pressure is too high. You may be given some form of medication. The doctor will advise you watch your weight and avoid too much alcohol. You will also be advised to cut down on salt.

To reduce salt intake

Avoid salted meat and salted fish. Use herbs, lemon juice or spices in cooking instead of salt. Cook vegetables in a very little water or steam or microwave them to reduce the salt required.

Try a low-salt product but check you can eat this; diabetics cannot, for instance.

Heart disease

This is a serious matter and you should follow all advice from your medical adviser. You will be urged to keep slim; to relax and may well be told to follow a low cholesterol diet.

Understanding cholesterol

It is believed that coronary heart disease can be caused by too much cholesterol in the blood. We produce this fat-like substance in our bodies naturally. Foods can affect this, but it is the amount and type of fats that are more important.

Fats are divided into different groups. Saturated fatty acids: tend to raise blood cholesterol. They are nearly all of animal origin: butter, cream, cheese, lard, suet, meat fats, dripping, etc. but some margarines also contain them.

Mono-unsaturated fatty acids: neither raise nor lower cholesterol. These are mostly in olives and olive oil; peanuts and peanut oil and avocados.

Polyunsaturated fatty acids: help to lower blood cholesterol. These are usually of vegetable origin, such as corn, rape seed, safflower, soya, sunflower seed oils. Some margarines and a new cooking fat are also polyunsaturated.

Foods and cholesterol

As well as selecting fats wisely, choose:– plenty of vegetables and fruit of all kinds; fish, for fish oils are believed to lower the cholesterol, as are foods containing dietary fibre (see page 131); chicken and turkey are ideal meats. Buy skimmed milk, low fat yogurt, cottage and low fat cheeses. *Avoid:* egg yolks, brains, hearts, liver, sweetbreads, tongue, tripe, shellfish (except lobster and scampi), and fish roes.

Being overweight

This is a health hazard that can stop you enjoying exercise and make you tire easily. We need rather less food as we get older, but it must be the right kind of food. Do not omit energy foods and those rich in calcium or vitamins, especially vitamin C (see pages 130 and 131).

If you have a diet sheet from the doctor follow this carefully. If you have just a little weight to lose cut down on alcohol, fats and sugars, all high in calories. Foods high in fibre make you feel 'full up'.

Check the calorific value of prepared foods you buy. The term 'Kilocalorie', also given as Kcalorie or calorie, is used to describe the energy value of the food we eat. Both terms are given in this book.

Pulses are an invaluable source of protein and dietary fibre

ESSENTIAL FOODS

The energy-giving foods are divided into 3 groups – proteins, fats and carbohydrates. We should eat some from each group daily.

The role of proteins

These are the main body building foods, they produce healthy growth in children and maintain and repair tissues in adults.

Protein is provided by meats, poultry, fish, cheese, eggs, milk, nuts, beans, peas and lentils. It is in grains like wheat and rice and in some seeds. Avocados and Brussels sprouts have some.

In the Western world we eat an adequate amount of protein foods. In fact, as we get older we are wise to limit our intake, particularly of red meat. Eat meat on 3 or 4 days and choose fish or poultry or vegetable proteins the rest of the week.

The role of fat

Fat is an important food, for it gives the most concentrated form of energy. This is why it is high in calories. While we must not omit fat completely (unless following a medical fat-free diet) it is advisable to reduce it. The average diet contains 42% fat, including margarine, oil and the fat from fish, meat, etc.

The ideal proportion of fat in the total diet should be from 30% to a MAXIMUM of 35%.

Easy ways to reduce fat intake

a) instead of cream, choose low fat foods, such as yogurt or fromage frais; the latter is fermented milk and contains only 45 calories for 100 g/ just under 4 oz.

Skimmed milk has only half the calories of full-cream milk. It is inclined to stick to the pan, so in sauces use the All-in-One Method (see page 75) or choose a non-stick pan or double saucepan or microwave.

Use one of the low-fat spreads on bread or for some cooking, as in a sauce (page 75) or crumble (page 78) and dumplings.
Low-fat Dumplings: Sift 100 g/4 oz self-raising flour, or plain flour and 1 teaspoon baking powder, with pinch of salt. Rub in 25 to 50 g/1 to 2 oz low fat spread. Mix with water to a soft rolling consistency. Form into about 8 small balls with floured hands. Cook in boiling stock or add to a stew.
b) change cooking methods – marinate foods, as on pages 39, 51 and 59, instead of using fat. Bake, grill or use microwave cooker and non-stick pans to save fat; cook foods in foil (see page 40).
c) choose recipes that have been created to use little fat; there are many in this book.

Shopping for fats

The array of fats can be confusing. All the following can be used for cooking as well as spreading. The letter 'S' means saturated fat; the letter 'P' polyunsaturated; where both letters are given check labels well. Butter (S); hard margarine (S); soft margarine (P, some S); dairy spreads (S); low-fat spreads (S and P); lard (S); cooking fats (S, rarely P); oils (see pages 128 and 122); very low-fat spreads – not for cooking (S).

The role of carbohydrates

These are divided into starches and sugars. Both provide quick energy and are digested rapidly. Starches are present in flour and goods made from flour, like bread and pasta, in potatoes, peas and beans.

Sugar is high in calories and does not supply essential nutrients, so reduce. Sugars include honey, syrup, treacle. Sugar substitutes are now much improved.

The role of minerals

These are present in most foods we eat. Two minerals are particularly important.

○ Calcium: as we grow older our bones become less dense and more likely to break. Older women in particular suffer from brittle bones and need adequate supplies of calcium. *Present* in: milk, cheese, yogurt, bread and also the bones from canned sardines and salmon. Vitamin D enables the body to absorb calcium.

○ Iron: prevents tiredness and even anaemia. *Present in*: red meats, liver, kidneys, peas, beans, lentils, cocoa, wholegrain cereals, dried fruits, many green vegetables.

The role of vitamins

These are not foods, but the protective element in food.

○ Vitamin A: helps to keep a healthy skin and eyes. It also protects the linings of the nose, mouth, ears and aids digestion. *Present in:* liver, fish liver oil, oily fish like herrings, egg yolk, butter, cheese, margarine, unskimmed milk, soya beans, carrot, green vegetables and some fruits.

○ Vitamin B group: these aid digestion, maintain energy, help to prevent muscular disease, nervous disorder and anaemia. *Present in:* wheatgerm (more of this in wholemeal foods than in white), in brewer's yeast, yeast extract (Marmite), liver, hearts, brains. To a lesser degree you find them in peas, beans, egg yolk, nuts, yogurt and unskimmed milk.

○ Vitamin C: also known as ascorbic acid; an essential vitamin. It helps to keep the skin and gums in good order. It is valuable in building up resistance to illness and helps the body absorb iron. *Present in:* citrus fruit (oranges etc.) berry fruits (such as strawberries). In green vegetables, but destroyed by overcooking. Have foods with vitamin C each day.

○ Vitamin D: essential for the body to absorb calcium and keep bones and teeth healthy. The main source is sunlight, so seek this when possible. *Present in*: fish liver oil, oily fish, egg yolk, butter, margarine, milk; is added to some breakfast cereals.

○ Vitamin E: helps to maintain healthy muscles. *Present in:* wheatgerm, green vegetables, seeds.

○ Vitamin F: helps to maintain health and absorb calcium and other vitamins. *Present in:* vegetables, oils and whole grains.

○ Vitamin K: helps calcium ensure healthy clotting of blood to stop undue bleeding. *Present in*: leafy green vegetables.

The role of fibre

Dietary fibre plays an important part in preventing constipation and ailments of the bowels, coronary heart disease, overweight, diverticulitis and even varicose veins.

An important source of fibre is bran, that is why we are urged to eat wholemeal foods for they are rich in bran. Wholemeal bread has 3 times as much fibre as white.

Cereals, oats in particular, fruit and vegetables supply fibre. There is more fibre if you eat an apple or orange, rather than having just the juice. The pulses – peas, beans and lentils – are sources of fibre as well as protein.

○ Insoluble fibre: helps the passage of food through the body. As it absorbs liquid, you should also drink plenty of water.

○ Soluble fibre: has been proved to be of benefit to diabetics; it plays a part in eliminating cholesterol from the body, so helps to prevent coronary heart disease. Oats and oat bran are major sources.

Although dietary fibre is so important never consume vast quantities without asking the doctor's advice.

LET'S ENTERTAIN

One of the pleasures of life is meeting friends or members of the family who no longer live at home. This chapter deals with those happy occasions and gives recipes for a variety of dishes. You will find menus and recipes for dinner parties and luncheon parties with information about preparing ahead, so you do not feel rushed or over-worked.

There are ideas, too, for less formal times, when you invite a friend to take 'pot luck'. The recipes will help you to produce a pleasant and speedy meal from the food you have in the house.

The visit of grandchildren is an occasion that grandparents cherish; and if you like to produce special 'goodies' there are recipes for these. Most of the food can be made ahead and stored ready for the visit.

It is sensible to keep both the freezer and storecupboard reasonably well stocked, so that last-minute shopping and cooking is not essential. It is interesting to find, as one gets older, that the circle of family and friends becomes very wide and falls into a whole range of age groups.

The first recipes here are for younger people. If very small they will enjoy a teatime meal. When almost adult they will appreciate your 'with it' approach to the informal food they generally prefer. Have a good range of soft drinks with non-alcoholic wine.

There are several menus in this chapter for interesting luncheon and dinner parties, plus tips to make the occasion run smoothly with the minimum of effort on the part of the cook. Suggestions for suitable wines are included.

For easy entertaining ask friends to join you for tea or coffee in the morning or later in the evening after you have had supper.

Maryland spaghetti (top) and Celery and cheese dip (recipes page 135)

THE YOUNGER GENERATION

Young people enjoy informal food, so they will approve of the recipes that follow. They like pasta dishes and pizzas (see pages 102 and 103) and food with a Chinese touch. A good percentage of the young are vegetarian, so cheese dishes will be popular.

PRINCESS CHICKEN

For the pasta layer:
75 g/3 oz quick cooking macaroni
salt and pepper
40 g/1½ oz butter or margarine
40 g/1½ oz flour or 20 g/¾ oz cornflour
300 ml/½ pint chicken stock (see page 48)
225 ml/7½ fl oz milk or use a mixture of milk
    and single cream
100 g/4 oz cooked peas
For the chicken layer:
550 g/1¼ lb cooked chicken (see page 64)
    cut into neat thin slices
50 g/2 oz Gruyère or Cheddar cheese,
    grated
150 ml/¼ pint whipping cream
50 g/2 oz soft breadcrumbs

Cook the macaroni in boiling salted water for approximately 8 minutes or until 'al dente', that is, firm to the bite and not oversoft. Strain the macaroni and put on one side. Heat the butter or margarine in a saucepan, stir in the flour or cornflour and stir over a low heat for several minutes. Add the stock and milk or milk and cream. Stir as the sauce comes to the boil and thickens. Add the macaroni, peas, salt and pepper to taste. Preheat the oven to moderate (180°C, 350°F, Gas Mark 4).

Spoon the macaroni into a 1.2 litre/2 pint casserole. Top with the sliced chicken. Blend the cheese and cream with the breadcrumbs. Spoon over the chicken; make sure this is completely covered with the cheese and cream mixture.

Heat for 25 to 30 minutes in the pre-heated oven.
Serves 4

For the busy cook: This can be prepared earlier in the day and heated in the microwave cooker for about 10 minutes on **Reheat** setting.

FREEZING: The cooked dish freezes well for up to 1 month.

SAVOURY CHEESECAKE

Cheese pastry made with 100 g/4 oz flour
    etc. (see page 121)
For the filling:
350 g/12 oz curd cheese
150 ml/¼ pint soured cream
1 tablespoon lemon juice
salt and pepper
12 stuffed olives, sliced
1 green and 1 red pepper, deseeded and
    cut into small dice
2 sticks celery, finely chopped

Preheat the oven to hot (200°C, 400°F, Gas Mark 6). Roll out the pastry to make a 20 to 23 cm/8 to 9 inch round. Place on a baking sheet and prick with a fork. Bake in the centre of the oven for 15 minutes or until golden brown; allow to cool.

Blend the cheese with all the ingredients except a few sliced olives. Spread over the pastry, top with the olives and chill. Serve with a salad or cut into small slices to serve with a drink.
Serves 4–6

CELERY AND CHEESE DIP

100 g/4 oz Cheddar or Gruyère cheese,
  grated
100 g/4 oz Stilton or other blue cheese,
  crumbled
4 tablespoons mayonnaise
3 tablespoons natural yogurt
salt and pepper
½–1 small celery heart, finely sliced
To serve with the dip:
celery, raw carrots, radishes

Put the cheeses into a bowl and blend well with a wooden spoon. Add the mayonnaise and yogurt. Season, then mix in the celery.

Cut the celery and carrots into 5 cm/ 2 inch pieces; leave a little stalk on the radishes and arrange all the prepared vegetables round the dip.

CHINESE-STYLE GRILLED FISH

For the marinade:
4 tablespoons white wine or dry sherry
2 tablespoons lemon juice
2 tablespoons oil
3 tablespoons soy sauce
1.5 cm/½ inch piece fresh ginger, chopped
1 garlic clove, crushed

4 portions white fish or 4 small trout

Blend all the ingredients for the marinade. Add the fish and leave for 2 hours.

Preheat the grill and line the grill pan with foil. Lift the fish from the marinade and place on the foil. Cook for 8 to 12 minutes, depending on the thickness of the fish. Moisten with the marinade and turn thick portions of fish over during cooking.
Serves 4

MARYLAND SPAGHETTI

225 g/8 oz spaghetti
salt and pepper
4 sausages
4 bacon rashers
1 × 425 g/15 oz can sweetcorn
25 g/1 oz butter or margarine
For the topping:
grated cheese
chopped parsley

Cook the spaghetti in plenty of boiling salted water; ideally, you need 2.5 litres/ 4 pints for this amount of pasta. Strain the spaghetti when it is just 'al dente', that is, firm to the bite and not oversoft. Meanwhile grill the sausages until brown and grill the bacon until crisp. Slice the sausages, chop the bacon.

Drain the canned sweetcorn, discarding the liquid. Heat the butter or margarine in the saucepan in which the spaghetti was cooked. Add the sweetcorn, heat for 2 or 3 minutes then add the spaghetti, sausages and bacon. When piping hot serve topped with grated cheese and parsley.
Serves 4

For the busy cook: Prepare everything ahead. To reheat, heat the butter or margarine, add the sweetcorn, plus 2 tablespoons of milk then put in the spaghetti, sausages and bacon and turn together until piping hot.

If more convenient, put all the ingredients except the butter or margarine into a casserole. Melt the butter or margarine, add 3 tablespoons milk. Pour over the spaghetti mixture. Cover the casserole and heat for 25 minutes in a moderate oven (180°C, 350°F, Gas Mark 4).

WITH A SWEET TOOTH

The desserts on this page are slightly unusual. The Victoria Sandwich mixture (page 124), can be used to make about 36 little cakes (any surplus can be frozen). Bake in greased patty tins or paper cases for 10 to 12 minutes at 200°C, 400°F, Gas Mark 6. When cold top with Glacé (water) icing: use 150 g/5 oz icing sugar; for 36 small cakes use 225 g/8 oz. Sift the sugar into a basin. Add 1¼ to 2 tablespoons water or fruit juice to make a spreading consistency.

HIGHLAND TART

Sweet shortcrust pastry made with 100 g/ 4 oz flour etc. as page 121
For the filling:
50 g/2 oz butter or margarine
50 g/2 oz soft light brown sugar
1 egg
50 g/2 oz rolled oats
25 g/1 oz currants
25 g/1 oz sultanas
25 g/1 oz candied peel, chopped
25 g/1 oz glacé cherries, chopped
25 g/1 oz blanched flaked almonds

Preheat the oven to moderately hot (190–200°C, 375–400°F, Gas Mark 5–6). Roll out the pastry thinly and line an 8 cm/7 inch flan dish or tin.

Cream the butter or margarine with the sugar, add the egg and mix well. Blend in the rest of the ingredients except the almonds. Spoon into the pastry and top with the almonds. Bake for 15 minutes; lower the heat to moderate (180°C, 350°F, Gas Mark 4) for a further 15 minutes.
Serves 4

PRALINE APPLE PIE

50 g/2 oz seedless raisins
2 tablespoons sweet sherry
600 ml/1 pint thick unsweetened apple purée
25 g/1 oz butter or margarine, melted
50 g/2 oz light brown sugar
3 eggs
50–75 g/2–3 oz praline*
75 g/3 oz caster sugar
25 g/1 oz blanched flaked almonds

*obtainable from confectioner's or substitute brittle toffee if not available.

Add the raisins to the sherry and leave to soak for 1 hour. Blend the raisins and any sherry left with the apple purée, butter or margarine.

Preheat the oven to cool (150°C, 300°F, Gas Mark 2).

Separate the eggs, beat the yolks into the apple mixture. Spoon into a fairly deep flan dish measuring 21.5–23 cm/8½–9 inches in diameter. Bake for 45 to 50 minutes or until firm. Meanwhile, crush the praline, sprinkle half over the top of the apple mixture.

For the meringue: whip the egg whites until very stiff. Gradually fold in the caster sugar. Spoon the meringue over the apple base and praline.

Lower the oven temperature to 140°C, 275°F, Gas Mark 1 and bake the dessert for 30 to 35 minutes. Top with the remaining praline and almonds. Serve hot.
Serves 4

For the busy cook: Prepare all the ingredients, bake the base ahead and freeze if desired. Thaw out, top with the meringue and continue as recipe.

Praline apple pie (left) and Highland tart (recipes this page)

UNEXPECTED GUESTS

These dishes can be prepared easily and quickly. If fresh ingredients are not available, use frozen or canned foods.

Menu 1

Orange Ginger Sardines, Kidneys Bercy, Russian Blinis (page 99) or a Yogurt Dessert (page 82). Use double the amounts of these recipes for 4 servings. Choose a Spanish or Chilean red wine.

Menu 2

Pears in Walnut and Watercress Sauce, Sweet and Sour Lamb, cheese and biscuits or Poor Knights' Fritters. It is not easy to 'match' wines with the flavours here but a chilled rosé or sparkling rosé is good.
NOTE: If no lamb is available use canned or cooked ham or tongue.

ORANGE GINGER SARDINES

8 fresh sardines
8 tablespoons orange juice
½ teaspoon ground ginger
To garnish:
watercress, orange wedges

Fresh sardines are large and plump and make an excellent light main dish. They do not require any extra fat for cooking.

Marinate the fish for an hour in the orange juice and ginger. Drain well and place the fish on a foil-lined grill pan. Cook for 7 to 8 minutes, moistening the fish with the remaining orange and ginger.
Serves 4

VARIATIONS:
Garlic and Tomato Sardines: Use tomato juice and a crushed garlic clove or a few drops of garlic liquid instead of the orange juice and ginger.
Using canned sardines: Drain the oil from the fish; blot the sardines on absorbent kitchen paper. Continue as the recipe.

KIDNEYS BERCY

8 lambs' kidneys
50 g/2 oz butter or margarine
2–3 bacon rashers, derinded and chopped
2 medium onions, finely chopped or grated
½ tablespoon lemon juice
salt and pepper
1 teaspoon paprika
150 ml/¼ pint dry white wine
1 tablespoon chopped parsley
1 teaspoon Worcestershire sauce

Wash the kidneys in cold water, remove the skins then halve the kidneys and cut away the white fat. Heat the butter or margarine with the bacon rinds. Add the onions and cook for 5 minutes, then add the halved kidneys and cook for 4 minutes, being careful not to overcook. Add the bacon and continue cooking for a further 3 minutes.

Remove the bacon rinds and then blend in the remaining ingredients. Heat thoroughly, stirring well until all the ingredients are blended. Serve with rice and salad.
Serves 4

VARIATION:
You can use canned kidneys in this dish. Cook the onions as the recipe then add the bacon and continue cooking. Finally add the remaining ingredients, plus the canned kidneys and heat thoroughly.

PEARS IN WALNUT AND WATERCRESS SAUCE

For the dressing:
1 tablespoon corn oil
1 tablespoon lemon juice
½ teaspoon French mustard
150 ml/¼ pint natural yogurt
salt and pepper
4 tablespoons chopped watercress leaves

lettuce leaves
2 large ripe dessert pears
4 tablespoons cottage or curd cheese
4 tablespoons coarsely chopped walnuts

Blend the ingredients for the dressing. Place a few lettuce leaves on small plates. Halve the pears, then peel and core them. Fill the hollows with the cheese then place on the lettuce with the rounded side uppermost. Coat with all the dressing and top with the walnuts.
Serves 4

SWEET AND SOUR LAMB PILAU

For the savoury lemon coating:
1 tablespoon corn or soya oil
1½ tablespoons lemon juice
½ teaspoon ground ginger
½ teaspoon ground or grated nutmeg
1 tablespoon honey

350 g/12 oz cooked lamb, cut into 2.5 cm/
    1 inch dice
225 g/8 oz brown or white long-grain rice
salt and pepper
25 g/1 oz butter or margarine
2 tablespoons seedless raisins
2 tablespoons blanched flaked almonds or
    pine nuts (optional)

Mix the ingredients for the lemon coating in a bowl. Add the lamb, turning until it is well covered. Cook the rice in salted water until just tender (see page 144), strain if any liquid remains. Heat the butter or margarine in a saucepan, add the meat, plus any coating in the bowl, the rice, raisins and nuts. Stir over a low heat until well heated.
Serves 4

For the busy cook: Prepare the meat and cook the rice earlier. Heat the ingredients just before the meal in a saucepan or covered dish in the oven. If using the oven add 2 tablespoons white wine or chicken stock to the ingredients so they do not dry.

MICROWAVE: The ingredients can be heated on **Full Power** in a covered dish for 3–4 minutes. Add 1 tablespoon white wine or chicken stock.

POOR KNIGHTS' FRITTERS

8 slices of bread
butter or margarine
jam or marmalade
For the coating:
1 egg
2 tablespoons milk
caster sugar

50 g/2 oz butter or margarine, for frying

Make sandwiches of the bread, butter or margarine and jam or marmalade. Cut into triangles. Beat the egg, milk and 1 teaspoon sugar. Heat the butter or margarine in a frying pan. Dip the sandwiches quickly into the egg mixture. Fry until crisp and brown on both sides. Drain on absorbent paper. Top with the sugar. Serve hot.
Serves 4

A LIGHT LUNCH MENU

Cucumber Sorbet (see page 143), Mussels Normandy with salad, Raspberry Syllabub. Choose a chilled white wine such as Sancerre or Riesling. Australian wines are worth considering.

MUSSELS NORMANDY

2.4 litres/4 pints mussels
150 ml/¼ pint water
150 ml/¼ pint white wine or extra water with
   1 tablespoon lemon juice
small bunch of parsley
1 onion, finely chopped or grated
salt and pepper
75 g/3 oz butter or margarine
100 g/4 oz small button mushrooms, sliced
50 g/2 oz plain flour
300 ml/½ pint milk
150 ml/¼ pint single cream
50 g/2 oz peeled prawns
2 tablespoons chopped parsley

Wash and clean the mussels in cold water. Discard any that are open and do not close when sharply tapped. Put into a large saucepan with the water and wine or lemon juice, the parsley, onion and a shake of pepper. Heat for approximately 5 minutes or until the mussels open. Strain and save the liquid. Discard any mussels that do not open. When cold remove the fish from the shells.

Heat 25 g/1 oz of the butter or margarine, add the mushrooms and cook for 2 minutes. Lift out of the pan. Heat the remaining butter or margarine in the same pan, stir in the flour; add the milk and cream. Stir or whisk until the sauce thickens then add the reserved cooking liquid. Heat until well blended then stir in the mussels, mushrooms, prawns, seasoning and chopped parsley. Heat for a few minutes. Serve with cooked rice.

Serves 4 as a main course, 6 as an hors d'oeuvre

For the busy cook: Prepare the mussels, the mushrooms and the sauce. Add the mussels, prawns and mushrooms to the *cool* sauce (this prevents the fish being overcooked by standing in a hot sauce). Cover with buttered paper and store in the refrigerator. Reheat just before serving.

RASPBERRY SYLLABUB

350 g/12 oz raspberries
2 tablespoons sweet sherry
50 g/2 oz caster sugar
150 ml/¼ pint whipping cream
150 ml/¼ pint natural or raspberry
   flavoured yogurt
½–1 tablespoon lemon juice

Put a few whole raspberries on one side for decoration. Mash or sieve or liquidize the remaining fruit, then blend with the sherry and sugar. Whip the cream until it just holds its shape. Save a little for decoration then fold the rest and the yogurt into the mashed raspberries. Add the lemon juice. Spoon into 4 glasses. Top with the remaining whipped cream and raspberries. Chill.
Serves 4

VARIATIONS:
Use other ripe fruit such as strawberries, redcurrants, ripe cherries or kiwifruit. A purée of cooked fruit can be used.

Raspberry syllabub (top) and Mussels Normandy, served with saffron rice (recipes this page)

DINNER PARTY DISHES

The recipes give dishes for 2 entirely different menus. The first is for people who enjoy sustaining dishes, the second to please guests who prefer lighter fare.

Menu 1
Kipper Pâté, using double the recipe quantities for 4 servings (page 24), Chicken Hotpot, Rhubarb Meringue Bake. Choose a light red wine like a Valpolicella.

Menu 2
Melon and Ginger Sorbet, Madeira Sweetbreads, Peasant Girl in a Veil, using double the recipe quantities for 4 servings (page 83). Choose a Spanish Rioja red wine.

CHICKEN HOT POT

3–4 bacon rashers, derinded and chopped
50 g/2 oz margarine
2 large onions, cut into thin rings
4 chicken legs
4 large tomatoes, skinned and sliced
2 tablespoons finely chopped parsley
1 teaspoon finely chopped thyme
150 ml/¼ pint chicken stock
2 tablespoons sherry
salt and pepper
450 g/1 lb potatoes, thinly sliced

Preheat the oven to moderate (180°C, 350°F, Gas Mark 4).

Heat the bacon rinds with 25 g/1 oz margarine and cook the onions for 5 minutes, add the diced bacon and cook for a further 2 minutes. Remove from the pan.

Blend the chicken joints with the tomatoes, onion and bacon. Put into a casserole.

Stir the parsley and thyme into the chicken stock and add the sherry and a little salt and pepper. Pour over the chicken. Arrange the sliced potatoes over the chicken mixture. Melt the remaining margarine, and spread or brush over the potatoes.

Bake the uncovered hot pot in the centre of the oven for 20 minutes; then lower the heat to 160°C, 325°F, Gas Mark 3, put on the lid and bake for 1¼ hours. Remove the lid again for the last 15 minutes.

Serve with pickled walnuts or red cabbage and a green vegetable.
Serves 4

RHUBARB MERINGUE BAKE

For the base:
450 g/1 lb rhubarb, weight when prepared
2 tablespoons orange juice
25–50 g/1–2 oz Demerara sugar
For the pudding:
1 large orange
75 g/3 oz butter or margarine
75 g/3 oz Demerara or caster sugar
2 eggs yolks
150 g/5 oz self-raising flour or plain flour
    sifted with 1¼ teaspoons baking powder
For the meringue:
2 egg whites
50 g/2 oz caster sugar
2 tablespoons blanched flaked almonds

Wash the rhubarb in cold water and dry well then cut the sticks into 2.5 cm/1 inch lengths. Put into the bottom of a 20 cm/8 inch soufflé dish or casserole. Add the orange juice and required amount of Demerara sugar, stir to mix with the rhubarb.

To make the pudding: Grate the top 'zest' from the orange, halve the fruit and squeeze out 3 tablespoons orange juice. Cream the butter or margarine, orange rind and sugar until soft and light; beat in the egg yolks then add the flour, or flour and baking powder, and the orange juice. Spread the mixture evenly over the rhubarb. Preheat the oven to 160°C, 325°F, Gas Mark 3. Bake in the centre of the oven for approximately 50 minutes or until firm to the touch, then remove from the oven. Lower the oven to 150°C, 300°F, Gas Mark 2.

Whisk the egg whites, fold in the sugar. Spoon the meringue over the pudding, top with the almonds and replace in the oven. Cook for 30 minutes then serve hot.
Serves 6

For the busy cook: Make the pudding earlier then top with the meringue just before the meal.

MADEIRA SWEETBREADS

550 g/1 1/4 lb calf's or lamb's sweetbreads
25 g/1 oz butter
25 g/1 oz plain flour
300 ml/1/2 pint chicken stock
150 ml/1/4 pint Madeira
2 medium onions, finely chopped or grated
3–4 tender celery sticks, cut in thin pieces
3 carrots, cut into thin sticks
salt and pepper

Soak the sweetbreads in cold water for 1 hour. Strain and put into a pan of cold water, bring the water to the boil and boil for 2 minutes then strain. This 'blanching' ensures the sweetbreads are a good flavour. Now preheat the oven to moderate (160°C, 325°F, Gas Mark 3).

Remove the skin and gristle from the sweetbreads. Heat the butter, add the flour and the chicken stock. Stir as the sauce thickens, add the Madeira and vegetables. Bring the sauce to the boil once more. Finally, add the sweetbreads and season-

ing. Put into a casserole, cover and cook for 1 hour in the oven.
Serves 4

MELON AND GINGER SORBET

150 ml/1/4 pint water
50 g/2 oz sugar
1 teaspoon ground ginger
1 large ripe honeydew melon
1–2 tablespoons lemon juice
2 egg whites (optional; see NOTE below)

Heat the water and sugar until the sugar has dissolved. Allow to cool then blend in the ginger. Halve the melon, remove the seeds then scoop out the pulp. Mash, sieve or liquidize the pulp then blend it with the ginger syrup. Add lemon juice to taste.

Lightly freeze the mixture until 'mushy'. Remove from the freezer. Whisk the egg whites until stiff, fold into the half-frozen mixture and return to the freezer.

This sorbet keeps for a week or two. Take from the freezer 20 minutes before serving.
Serves 4–6

VARIATIONS:
Apple and Lemon Sorbet: Use cooked apple purée instead of melon purée and a rather more generous amount of lemon juice. Omit the ginger.
Cucumber Sorbet: Omit the sugar syrup. Make a purée from a large peeled cucumber. Flavour this with lemon juice and seasoning then freeze. Serve topped with natural yogurt and mint leaves.
NOTE: As the egg whites are uncooked, it is important to check on medical opinion regarding these. The sorbet is very pleasant if the whites are omitted.

TOUCH OF CURRY

The main dish in this menu is lightly flavoured with curry. You could, of course, substitute veal or lamb chops for the pork.

Menu
Avocado and Grapefruit Cocktails using double the recipe quantities for 4 servings (see page 23), Devilled Pork Chops with Harlequin Rice, cheese and biscuits with celery. The light curry flavour will not spoil the taste of a well chilled rosé or white wine, but cold beer could be offered.

DEVILLED PORK CHOPS

4 large loin pork chops
For the topping:
1–2 teaspoons dry mustard powder,
    depending upon personal taste
½–1 teaspoon curry powder
6 tablespoons crisp breadcrumbs
3 teaspoons corn, soya or other oil
pinch cayenne pepper
For the sauce:
25 g/1 oz margarine
2 medium onions, finely chopped or grated
15 g/½ oz plain flour
1 teaspoon dry mustard powder
1 teaspoon curry powder
300 ml/½ pint chicken stock (see page 48)
1 teaspoon Worcestershire sauce
salt and pepper

Grill the pork chops until nearly, but not quite cooked, remove from the pan and drain well on absorbent kitchen paper. Cut away the rind and any surplus fat. Blend the ingredients for the topping together and press over one side of the chops.

Make the sauce: heat the margarine in a pan, add the onions and turn in the hot fat. Blend in the flour, mustard powder and curry powder then gradually blend in the chicken stock. Stir as the sauce comes to the boil and thickens slightly. Lower the heat. Cover the pan tightly and simmer gently for 15 minutes. Add the Worcestershire sauce, with salt and pepper to taste.

To complete the dish: either reheat the chops steadily under the grill set at medium heat or place them in an ovenproof dish with the coated side uppermost and cook in a moderately hot oven (200°C, 400°F, Gas Mark 6) for 15 to 20 minutes. Serve the chops with the sauce.
Serves 4

For the busy cook: Prepare both the chops and sauce. Reheat when required.

VARIATION:
Devilled Halibut: Choose cutlets of halibut or any other firm fleshed fish instead of meat. Use chicken stock in the sauce if you have no fish stock. The topping for fish is exactly as in the recipe for pork.

HARLEQUIN RICE

Measure out 1½ teacups of long-grain brown rice; put into a saucepan with 3 teacups cold water and salt to taste. Bring the water to the boil, stir. Cover the pan and simmer gently for 30 minutes or until the rice is just tender and the water has evaporated.

Add cooked peas, diced red and green pepper, drained canned sweetcorn. Heat in the pan or microwave when required.

Stuffed topside (top – recipe page 146) and Devilled pork chops with Harlequin rice (recipes this page)

BASED ON ROAST JOINTS

The vegetables for these, and the other menus in this chapter, are not detailed as they will vary according to the season.

Menu 1
Piquant Cauliflower Soup or Leek Consommé, using double the recipe quantities for 4 servings (see pages 30 and 31), Stuffed Topside, Coffee Raisin Cheesecake. Choose a really full-bodied red wine, such as an Italian Barolo★, the less heavy French Volnay★ or a Spanish red.★

Menu 2
Herbed Fish Pâté, Lamb Guard of Honour, Peach and Coconut Crumble (see page 78). A Volnay★ would be good as would a chilled rosé.
★Open red wines in all menus early.

STUFFED TOPSIDE

few drops oil
1 kg/2¼ lb topside of beef
For the stuffing:
25 g/1 oz margarine
1 medium onion, chopped or grated
100 g/4 oz mushrooms, chopped
50 g/2 oz soft wholemeal breadcrumbs
2 tablespoons chopped parsley
1 egg
salt and pepper

Spread a large piece of foil with the oil. Cut the joint into 3 slices vertically. Heat the margarine and add the onion and mushrooms; cook for 5 minutes then add the remainder of the ingredients. Sandwich the layers of beef together so returning the

joint to its original shape.

Preheat the oven to moderate (180°C, 350°F, Gas Mark 4). Wrap the beef loosely in the foil. Stand in a roasting tin and cook for 1¼ hours in the oven. Open the foil for the last 20 minutes.
Serves 4–6

VARIATION:
Instead of the mushrooms, use 175 g/6 oz cooked stoned prunes. Bind with prune juice instead of the egg.

COFFEE RAISIN CHEESECAKE

For the biscuit base:
175 g/6 oz digestive biscuits, crushed
50 g/2 oz butter or margarine, melted
25 g/1 oz caster sugar
For the filling:
100 g/4 oz seedless raisins
3 tablespoons Tia Maria or Kahlua (coffee flavoured liqueurs)
150 ml/¼ pint coffee (drinking strength)
75 g/3 oz soft brown sugar
15 g/½ oz gelatine
450 g/1 lb curd cheese
150 ml/¼ pint whipping cream
To decorate:
raisins (see method)
2–3 tablespoons chopped walnuts
little extra whipped cream

Blend the biscuits, butter or margarine and sugar. Put on one side.

Put the raisins into a dish with the coffee liqueur and leave to soak for an hour. Heat the coffee, add the brown sugar, stir until dissolved. Sprinkle the gelatine on to the sweetened coffee, stir until dissolved. Allow to cool, then gradually blend with the cheese. Spoon half the raisins out of the liqueur and set aside for decoration. Stir the

remaining raisins and any Tia Maria or Kahlua not absorbed by the dried fruit into the cheese and coffee mixture. Allow to stiffen slightly. Whip the cream until it just holds its shape, then fold into the other ingredients. Spoon the mixture into a 23 cm/9 inch cake tin with a loose base. Sprinkle the biscuit crumb mixture on top. Leave until set then invert on to a serving plate. Top with the raisins, nuts and cream.
Serves 6–8

VARIATION:
Use sieved cottage cheese and natural yogurt in place of curd cheese and whipped cream. Omit the cream decoration.

FREEZING: Like most cheesecakes, this freezes perfectly. Always allow **any** jellied mixture to set before freezing.

HERBED FISH PÂTÉ

100 g/4 oz cooked salmon (weight when cooked), finely flaked
100 g/4 oz peeled prawns, finely chopped
2 teaspoons chopped parsley
2 teaspoons chopped fennel leaves or chopped dill or chives
½–1 tablespoon lemon juice, or to taste
1 garlic clove, finely crushed or few drops garlic juice
50 g/2 oz butter or margarine, melted
1 tablespoon single or double cream or natural yogurt
salt and pepper
To garnish:
lemon wedges
lettuce

Simply mix the ingredients, except the garnish, together until well blended. You can put the pieces of salmon, prawns and the other ingredients into a food processor and process the mixture for a few seconds,

in which case it is unnecessary to flake the salmon or chop the herbs and garlic. Take care not to over-process the mixture as it will become unpleasantly sticky.

Spoon into individual containers, or a bowl and chill. Serve garnished with hot toast or crispbread.
Serves 4

VARIATIONS:
Cooked white fish, like turbot or halibut, make a delicious pâté.
Smoked salmon could be used in place of the fresh salmon or prawns. Often you can buy more economical little pieces of the smoked fish.

LAMB GUARD OF HONOUR

2 best ends (racks) of lamb, made into a Guard of Honour
For the apricot stuffing:
100 g/4 oz dried apricots, cooked and cut into strips (weight before cooking)
½ tablespoon lemon juice
1 dessert apple, peeled and grated
50 g/2 oz walnuts, chopped
50 g/2 oz wholemeal breadcrumbs
50 g/2 oz butter or margarine, melted
salt and pepper

Preheat the oven to moderately hot (190–200°C, 375–400°F, Gas Mark 5–6).

Weigh the meat, protect the ends of the bones with foil. Roast for 20 minutes per 450 g/1 lb and 20 minutes over in the preheated oven.

Mix the ingredients for the stuffing, put into a dish, cover and cook for 35 minutes.

Remove the foil, put cutlet frills on to the ends of the bones. Spoon a little stuffing in the centre, serve the rest separately.
Serves 4

FINISHING TOUCHES

This chapter deals with some of the enjoyable extras that will help to make your catering more varied and interesting. There are basic recipes for a number of preserves, plus ideas to vary them. These will help the housekeeping budget, for although they are expensive to buy, they are surprisingly economical to make.

Microwave cooking of preserves

If you are making small amounts of jam or other preserves use the microwave cooker. The proportions of fruit, sugar and lemon juice (if needed) are the same as when making the preserve in a pan, but you need only half the usual amount of water. The method is on page 151. When making chutney keep all quantities the same but reduce the vinegar by one third. Never use more than a **total weight** of 1.6 to 1.8 kg/3½ to 4 lb of the ingredients at one time and use a very large bowl. Be very careful how you handle this when it comes from the microwave; the contents are very hot.

Preserves without sugar

If you are on a diabetic diet use the sugar alternatives prescribed. If, on the other hand, you are just trying to cut down on your total sugar intake then use one of the modern sweeteners in granular form. As you will know, it is the pectin in the fruit that causes jam to set; sugar, however, is the important preservative. If you omit sugar make only small amounts of jam etc., which you will be able to use up fairly quickly, and store them in the refrigerator. Freeze larger quantities.

Using herbs

There has been a revival in the use of fresh herbs; they enhance the flavour of many dishes and also make attractive garnishes. Herbs are easily grown in the garden, in pots or in a window box.

Home-made confectionery

There are easy recipes on pages 155 and 156. Making sweets, like the other ideas in this chapter, could develop into a real hobby and become a good – and popular – way of raising money for charity or even a good source of pocket money.

Making your own preserves allows you to use less sugar and more fresh fruit

PRESERVES

It is important to choose ripe, but not over-ripe fruit. Prepare the fruit as for cooking. When cooking the fruit, simmer slowly – this extracts the pectin more efficiently than fast cooking. Make sure the fruit is soft before adding the sugar; this is important, for the fruit will not soften once the sugar is added. When adding the sugar, or sugar and lemon juice (if this is needed), stir well over a moderate heat until the sugar has dissolved, then allow the preserve to boil as rapidly as possible, **without** stirring. Stirring hinders setting. Use a large pan, or bowl in the microwave, so there is no fear of the preserve boiling over.

The proportion of fruit to sugar depends upon the amount of natural setting quality (pectin) in the fruit, e.g. if using fruit low in pectin (see Group 1 fruits) you need to use rather more fruit than sugar, plus lemon juice or the special sugar.

Choosing the sugar

Use preserving sugar, for this helps to prevent a scum forming. A sugar that contains pectin is now available, so use this for Group 1 fruits and omit the lemon juice.

Testing for setting point

Start testing early, for overcooking can prevent some preserves setting. Use one of the following ways:

1.) Use a sugar thermometer. Stir this around in the boiling preserve to get the overall temperature. Jams set at 104–105.5°C, 220–222°F, jellies at 104–105°C, 220–221°F.

2.) Take the pan away from the heat or turn off the heat. Put a little preserve on a saucer; allow to cool. Push with your finger or a spoon: the preserve should wrinkle.

3.) Take the pan away from the heat or turn the heat off. Stir a wooden spoon round in the hot preserve, so it is well coated. Cool and hold horizontally. The preserve should hang in a flake.

Putting into jars

Always heat the jars well in a container to facilitate easy removal from the oven on the lowest setting. Buy proper jam pot covers.

Carefully pour some of the preserve into a heat-resistant jug then pour into the jar to within 5 mm/¼ inch of the top. Put on the waxed circle and final cover. With whole fruit or marmalade, allow the preserve to cool until sticky, then put into pots.

Group 1 – fruit with little (low) pectin: fresh apricots★, blackberries, dessert cherries and plums★, strawberries.
Allow: 500 g/1 lb 2 oz fruit (weight when stoned) to each 450 g/1 lb sugar plus 1 tablespoon lemon juice. You may need 2 tablespoons water with apricots and plums.
Group 2 – fruit with average pectin: ripe damsons★, gooseberries, Morello cherries, loganberries, cooking plums★, raspberries, rhubarb.
Allow: 450 g/1 lb fruit to each 450 g/1 lb sugar. You need 4 tablespoons water for damsons, gooseberries and firm plums.
Group 3 – fruits high in pectin: cooking apples and gooseberries, firm damsons★, quinces, red and black currants.
Allow: 450 g/1 lb fruit to each 500 g/1 lb 2 oz sugar. Allow 4 tablespoons water or up to 300 ml/½ pint with firm fruit.
★ Add an extra 50 g/2 oz fruit to compensate for the weight of the stones which are removed during the cooking process.

Making jellies

The best fruits for jelly are those with a strong flavour, i.e. cooking or crab apples, black or red currants, but use any juicy fruits; see the groups on page 150. Add lemon juice with the sugar as directed below. There is no need to peel or stone fruit; simply chop it up if large. Simmer the fruit with the water until a pulp. Put through a jelly bag over a large bowl or place 2 or 3 thicknesses of muslin on a hair or nylon sieve over the bowl. *Do not use a metal sieve* as it spoils the taste; do not press the pulp, as this clouds the juice.

To each 600 ml/1 pint juice allow 450 g/1 lb sugar, plus 1 tablespoon lemon juice if the fruits belong to Group 1: see page 150. Proceed as for jam.

Herb jellies

Add 2 or 3 tablespoons finely chopped mint, sage or tarragon plus 2 teaspoons vinegar when the jelly has just reached setting point; boil for a minute. An apple or gooseberry jelly is ideal for this.

Microwave jams and jellies

Use a really large heat-proof bowl. Follow the directions on page 150 for the proportions of fruit, sugar and lemon juice. Reduce the water by half. Put the fruit, plus water (if required) into the bowl; cover and cook only until just soft. You can use Full power or Roast setting (approximately 66% output). Check carefully during cooking and stir once or twice if the fruit is cooking unevenly. Do not overcook.

Add the sugar and lemon juice (if needed), stir well to dissolve. If necessary, return the bowl to the microwave cooker and heat for 1 minute; stir again. Repeat this stage. Always set the microwave to Full power when the sugar has dissolved. Boil rapidly until the setting point is reached. Stir every 5 minutes. *Do not cover the bowl at this stage.*

MAKING MARMALADE

Undoubtedly this is one of the most economical preserves to make at home. If you find that cutting up the oranges before, or after, cooking is difficult, you may like to buy the canned chopped oranges.

450 g/1 lb Seville or bitter oranges
1.5 litres/2½ pints water
1.1 kg/2½ lb preserving or granulated
*   sugar*
2 tablespoons lemon juice

Halve the oranges, remove the pips and tie them in a piece of muslin. Chop the peel and pulp of the fruit in a mincer or food processor or with a sharp knife.

Place in a bowl with the water and bag of pips and soak for 12 hours. Tip the fruit and bag of pips into a preserving pan or large saucepan and simmer gently until the peel is tender. This takes at least 1½ hours. It is very important, for the peel never softens when once the sugar is added.

Remove the pips, stir in the sugar and continue stirring until the sugar has dissolved. Add the lemon juice. Allow the preserve to boil briskly until setting point is reached (see page 150). Cool slightly, stir and pour into jars then seal.
Makes 1.9 kg/4 lb 3 oz

VARIATIONS:
Simmer the oranges whole; when soft halve; remove pips. Simmer these in the liquid for 10 minutes, strain; return to the pan with the cut-up oranges, sugar and lemon juice.
Grapefruit Marmalade: As recipe above.
Sweet Orange, Lemon or Tangarine Marmalade: Use 1.2 litres/2 pints water, 900 g/2 lb sugar. Sweet oranges and tangerines also need 3 tablespoons lemon juice.

MAKING CHUTNEYS

Use a good malt vinegar and do not cook the preserve in a brass, copper or iron pan. Never place a metal lid over the chutney; glass-topped jars are ideal.

Instead of the apples or oranges in either recipe use red or green tomatoes, plums, rhubarb, fresh or soaked dried apricots.

If using a microwave follow the advice under Jams on page 151. If using sugar substitute follow the directions on the pack.

ORANGE AND APPLE CHUTNEY

450 g/1 lb sweet oranges, seedless if possible
225 g/8 oz onions, finely chopped or grated
450 ml/¾ pint white malt vinegar
450 g/1 lb cooking apples, weight when peeled, cored and sliced
300 g/10 oz granulated sugar
½ teaspoon salt
good shake cayenne pepper
175 g/6 oz seedless raisins

Remove the peel from the oranges, cut away and discard most of the white pith; check there are no pips in the oranges. Put the orange peel and the pulp through a mincer, making sure you keep all the juice. You can use a food processor to chop the peel and fruit finely.

Put the onions and vinegar into a saucepan. Cover this and simmer for 10 minutes then add the oranges. Allow to stand for an hour with the onions and vinegar; this reduces the cooking time and so retains more of the flavour of the fruit.

Return the pan to the heat with the apples, do not cover. Cook steadily for 10 to 15 minutes; stir in the sugar and continue stirring until dissolved. Boil for 10 minutes,

then add the remaining ingredients. Cook until the consistency of jam. Spoon into hot jars and cover (see Indian Relish, below). Makes approximately 1.25 kg/2¾ lb

INDIAN RELISH

450 g/1 lb cooking apples, weight when peeled
450 g/1 lb green tomatoes
450 ml/¾ pint white malt vinegar
350 g/12 oz granulated sugar
¼ teaspoon cayenne pepper, or to taste
½ teaspoon ground ginger
½ teaspoon salt

Chop the apples and tomatoes finely. Bring the vinegar and other ingredients to the boil, stir until the sugar dissolves; add the apples and tomatoes. Simmer steadily for 30 minutes or until thick. Spoon into heated jars. Seal with glass tops or line metal tops with thick rounds of white paper or with cardboard.
Makes 1.2 kg/2¾ lb

POTTED FOODS

These make ideal gifts. Use cheese; fish, like salmon; or meats such as bacon. Boil a small joint of gammon until tender; strain, save the stock for cooking. Grate cheese, flake cooked fish, mince cooked meat.

To each 350 g/12 oz of your chosen food allow 50 g/2 oz melted butter, 2 tablespoons sherry or port wine, seasoning and either a little ground cinnamon, lemon juice or chopped fresh herbs. Mix the ingredients together. Put into small containers, cover with melted butter and when cold cover tightly. Label 'To be eaten while fresh'.

Fresh herbs add wonderful flavours and aromas to many dishes and can be quite easy to grow

KNOW ABOUT HERBS

Even if you have no garden, you can still grow herbs in pots or a window box. If you do grow herbs in the garden and have a surplus of these, your friends will welcome bouquets of fresh herbs.

Learning about herbs is a fascinating subject. Below are some of the most useful.

'P' stands for perennial herbs which should come up each year, though many die back in winter. Initially you need to buy the plants.

'A' denotes an annual plant; you need to buy seeds each year and plant these as instructed. Use good potting compost.

○ Balm (P) This gives a lovely lemony aroma – so pleasant to grow. It is excellent in drinks of all kinds.

○ Basil (A) Add to tomato dishes; especially good in a tomato salad or sauce.

○ Bay (P) An expensive plant to buy; protect it well in winter. Use 1 or 2 leaves in a stew, sauce and milk pudding; remove these before serving the dish.

○ Borage (A) A slight cucumber taste. Use in sauces, fish dishes and soups. It is also used in drinks, particularly in Pimms.

○ Chives (P) This herb has a mild onion taste. Use in salads, egg and fish dishes.

○ Dill (A) A mild aniseed flavour. Use in fish or vegetable dishes and pickles.

○ Fennel (P) It is not easy to achieve the mature plant with the white base, but you will have the feathery leaves. The whole plant has an aniseed flavour. Use the leaves in fish dishes.

○ Garlic (A) A pungent onion flavour. Use 1 or 2 cloves only from the garlic head unless the recipe states otherwise. A garlic press extracts the juice. To chop garlic easily, put a little salt on the board.

○ Horseradish (P) The pungent root is used to make the famous sauce to serve with beef. Gardeners advocate digging up the mature root in winter, storing it in damp sand and planting small pieces of the root for a fresh crop in the spring.

○ Marjoram or Oregano (wild marjoram) (P) Ideal flavouring for pizza.

○ Mint (P) Invaluable with lamb for mint sauce, in salads and drinks. In a garden you could grow several kinds.

○ Parsley (A) This is a biennial though it is treated as an annual. Try and plant this to give continuity regularly.

○ Rosemary (P) A bush that looks attractive. Add a sprig when roasting lamb. Use the chopped leaves in salads.

○ Sage (P) this is a pungent herb. Use sparingly in stuffings, sauces and stews.

○ Tarragon (P) French tarragon is milder than the Russian type and more likely to die in winter. Use in fish dishes, salad dressings and vinegars.

○ Thyme (P) There are various kinds of thyme – try lemon thyme and the attractive golden thyme. Thyme has a mild flavour and is good in soups, stuffings and stews.

Preserving herbs

Wash the herbs; dry on absorbent paper.

To freeze: Chop the herbs. Either pack in small containers or put into ice-making trays, cover with water, and freeze.

To dry: Cover baking trays with brown paper and then muslin. Top with a flat layer of herbs. Dry in the sun, or in a heated airing cupboard or in the oven set at very low (90°C, 200°F, Gas Mark ¼) then chop.

Parsley is better prepared as above then dried for 3 minutes in a very hot oven (230°C, 450°F, Gas Mark 8). When brittle and cold, crumble or chop.

SWEETMEATS

If selling sweets, or giving them as presents, put them into individual paper cases then pack in attractive containers.
USING NUTS: these are mentioned in several recipes. All nuts are high in fat; the best nuts to choose for a low cholesterol diet are Brazils, cashews, hazelnuts, peanuts and walnuts. These all have a high amount of polyunsaturated fatty acids. Recipes that include coconut have a high amount of saturated fatty acids.

MIXED FRUIT TRUFFLES

50 g/2 oz glacé cherries
75 g/3 oz dried apricots, tenderised type if
   possible
50 g/2 oz dessert dates, weight when
   stoned
50 g/2 oz hazelnuts or blanched almonds
50 g/2 oz dried figs
75 g/3 oz seedless raisins
50 g/2 oz ground almonds
For the coating:
25 g/2 oz cocoa powder, sifted
25 g/1 oz icing sugar, sifted

Put the cherries, apricots, dates, nuts, figs and raisins through a mincer or into a food processor. Mince or process finely. Blend in the ground almonds. Form into small balls. Blend the cocoa and icing sugar in a plastic bag. Drop the small balls into the bag and shake until well coated.
Makes 50–60

VARIATION:
Coconut Fruit Truffles: Use desiccated coconut instead of ground almonds and 40–50 g/1½–2 oz desiccated coconut instead of cocoa for coating the truffles.

CHOCOLATE RUM TRUFFLES

24-36 glacé cherries
3 teaspoons rum
100 g/4 oz fine plain sponge cake crumbs
4 level tablespoons sieved apricot jam
25 g/1 oz chocolate powder, sifted
25 g/1 oz icing sugar, sifted
For the coating:
25 g/1 oz chocolate powder, sifted
25 g/1 oz icing sugar, sifted

Put the glacé cherries into a basin, add half the rum and stir so all the cherries absorb the flavour. Blend the rest of the rum with the cake crumbs, apricot jam, chocolate powder and icing sugar. Mix the ingredients very well. Divide into 24–36 portions, depending upon the number of cherries.

Remove the first cherry from the basin and roll the mixture around this. Continue until all the cherries are coated.

Blend the chocolate powder and icing sugar in a plastic bag. Add the truffles and shake very gently until coated.
Makes 24–36

UNCOOKED FONDANT

450 g/1 lb icing sugar, well sifted
2 large egg whites or the equivalent in dried
   egg white
2 teaspoons lemon juice
2 teaspoons glycerine

Blend the ingredients together and beat until white and shiny. In an electric mixer allow just 2 minutes on low speed; in a food processor allow barely ½ minute. The fondant should be a good consistency for handling.

Divide into 3 parts and use as follows.

Fondant Dates: Stone dessert dates, fill with a little fondant, roll in caster sugar.

Cherry and Walnut Balls: Work 50 g/2 oz chopped glacé cherries and 50 g/2 oz chopped walnuts into the fondant. Roll into small balls and coat in finely chopped walnuts.

Peppermint Creams: Work a few drops of peppermint essence or oil of peppermint into the fondant. If you have any cream, work just 1 teaspoon into the mixture. Roll the fondant on a board dusted with a little sifted icing sugar until it is 5 mm/¼ inch in thickness. Cut into 2.5 cm/1 inch rounds. Leave on the working surface while the creams harden on the outside.

Makes approx. 675 g/1½ lb in total

CREAMY FUDGE

150 ml/¼ pint water
1 × 397 g/14 oz can full cream sweetened condensed milk
50 g/2 oz unsalted butter
450 g/1 lb granulated sugar
½ teaspoon vanilla essence

It is important to use a thick saucepan as fudge has a tendency to burn in a thin pan. It needs stirring during cooking so make sure you have a really long-handled wooden spoon so you do not burn your fingers.

Grease a 20 cm/8 inch square sandwich tin with a little melted butter.

Put all the ingredients into the saucepan and stir over a low heat until the butter and sugar have dissolved. Boil steadily, stirring from time to time. The fudge is ready when it reaches 114°C/238°F. If you do not own a sugar thermometer have a bowl of cold water ready. Drop a little mixture into the water. The sweetmeat has reached the right temperature when it forms a mixture that can be rolled into a soft ball.

When you have reached the right stage, take the pan away from the heat and beat the fudge until it thickens slightly and becomes opaque (milky looking). This makes quite sure it is beautifully smooth.

Pour into the prepared tin and allow to set. Cut into small squares with a really sharp knife. Remove from the tin when quite cold.

Although the individual pieces of fudge do not need wrapping, it is better to put the sweets into a covered box or tin as exposure to the air makes them become less smooth.
Makes 675 g/1½ lb

VARIATIONS:
Extra Rich Fudge: Omit the condensed milk; use 300 ml/½ pint double cream instead. Use 150 ml/¼ pint milk instead of this measure of water. Add 3 tablespoons water. Follow the same method.

Coffee Fudge: Use 150 ml/¼ pint strong coffee in place of the water in the basic recipe or instead of the milk in the Extra Rich Fudge.

Chocolate Fudge: Blend 2 level tablespoons cocoa powder into the mixture after the sugar has melted.

Fruit Fudge: Add approximately 100 g/4 oz seedless raisins or sultanas to the fudge when setting point has been reached. You can add chopped nuts or glacé cherries.

MICROWAVE: The fudge can be cooked in a strong bowl in the microwave cooker on **Full power**. You must remove the bowl every 30 seconds and stir well until the sugar and butter have melted. After this allow the mixture to cook, stirring occasionally. Test as before. Be very careful not to put the bowl containing the very hot sweetmeat on a cold and damp surface when it finally comes from the cooker as it could crack.

INDEX

Acknowledgements

Special photography by Paul Grater
Food prepared for photography by Ricky Turner
Stylist, Marian Price

The following photographs, from the Octopus Group
Picture Library, were taken by: Martin Brigdale,
page 129; Paul Grater, page 93; Melvin Gray, pages 149, 153;
Gina Harris, pages 119, 123; Vernon Morgan, page 101;
Roger Phillips, page 15; Clive Streeter, page 11.
The author supplied the photograph on page 7.